WHAT'S LOVE GOT TO DO WITH IT?

Love, Power, Sex, and God

FRANK A. THOMAS
EDITED BY JINI KILGORE ROSS

Judson Press
Valley Forge

What's Love Got to Do with It? Love, Power, Sex, and God
© 2001 by Judson Press, Valley Forge, PA 19482-0851
All rights reserved.

Bible quotations in this volume are from *The Holy Bible*, King James Version (KJV); the New American Standard Bible (NASB), © 1960, 1962, 1963, 1968, 1971, 1972, 1973, 1975, 1977 by the Lockman Foundation, used by permission; the New King James Version (NKJV), copyright © 1972, 1984 by Thomas Nelson, Inc.; and HOLY BIBLE: *New International Version* (NIV), copyright © 1973, 1978, 1984, used by permission of Zondervan Bible Publishers.

Library of Congress Cataloging-in-Publication Data

Thomas, Frank A. (Frank Anthony), 1955-
    What's love got to do with it? : love, power, sex, and God / Frank A. Thomas; edited by Jini Kilgore Ross.
      p. cm.
    ISBN 0-8170-1391-1 (pbk. : alk. paper)
  1. Relationship addiction-Religious aspects-Christianity-Sermons. 2. Sermons, American-20th century. 3. Baptists-Sermons. I. Kilgore, Jini Ross. II. Title.

BV4596.R43 T48 2001
241'.66–dc21   00-060371

Printed in the U.S.A.

07 06 05 04 03 02 01

10 9 8 7 6 5 4 3 2

To my son, Tony, and my daughter, Rachel,
that you may learn years and years before I did
what love's got to do with it.

Contents

Foreword

Dr. Frank A. Thomas has tackled a very complex and complicated set of relationships in this volume of essays, developed from his sermon series, "What's Love Got to Do with It?" He uses the words and concepts of the song, sung by Tina Turner, to examine this culture's distorted and dysfunctional understandings of male-female relationships and the "power games" that are played between African American men and women.

It is Dr. Thomas's position that women and men need to take responsibility for their own lives. They need to take responsibility for the choices they make. They need to take responsibility for loving themselves first and for developing a personal relationship with the Lord before they start trying to enter into relationships with other persons.

Dr. Thomas argues quite cogently that based on the words of Jesus, it really is all right to love one's self. Jesus said, "Thou shalt love the Lord thy God with all thy heart, with all thy soul, with all thy strength, and with all thy mind; and thou shalt love thy neighbor as thyself."

Most of us feel guilty about loving ourselves, and that leads to all kinds of problems, especially relationship problems. A lack of love for one's self causes us to become "needy" and causes us to enter into relationships that we call "love relationships." Those relationships, however, are a far cry from what God had in mind when making us in the divine image. As the Reverend Frederick Douglas Haynes says, "If you don't like you, then what makes you think someone else is going to like you?"

Dr. Thomas's theological, philosophical, and homiletical points of departure will be jarring to many readers of this book. (Thomas himself uses the word "radical" when describing his points of departure.) I suspect that his points of departure will be jarring because they go against many of our "familiar" understandings of certain biblical texts.

I also suspect that they will be jarring because they will pull many readers out of their comfort zones and make us examine our own presuppositions and premises using an entirely different perspective and set of exegetical lenses.

This collection of essays can be used as a personal resource for believers. An engagement of the biblical texts that Dr. Thomas selects will be transformative for many who read this volume with an eye and a heart for seeing and hearing a "fresh word" from the Lord concerning those issues which consume most of our waking hours.

Dr. Thomas argues that the culture's emphasis on sex and sexuality causes most males to be consumed with sexual thoughts. Everything from beer commercials on television to movies, plays, and popular songs (from love ballads to hip-hop songs) revolves around sex, the power play between women and men, and the games that are played in order to "hit it and quit it!"

Because these sexual images consume our thoughts, we confuse sex with love and end up making bad choices and entering into terrible transactions which we mistakenly call love relationships!

In addition to being used as a personal resource for believers, this book can be used as a congregational resource. Women's groups and men's groups will find Dr. Thomas's probing questions and radical beliefs to be excellent topics for discussion starters, workshops, seminars, and Bible classes. In addition, the study questions for each chapter prepared by the Reverend Jini Kilgore Ross are excellent resources for getting discussions started within congregational groups. They will help stimulate conversations between males and females, and they will also be helpful for individual study and reflection-especially for those be-lievers who use journaling as a spiritual discipline.

The readers may not agree with many of Dr. Thomas's "beliefs," but an examination of those beliefs and an articulation of why there is agree-ment or disagreement will put the readers and the students in a new and a much healthier place in terms of their understanding of love, God, and sexuality.

Because there is such confusion among speakers of English as it per-tains to the word love, there is even greater confusion between and among African American women and men as to what is actually meant when one uses or hears that word. In the Greek language, for instance, the three words for love–eros, philos, and agape–respectively differen-tiate between the erotic feelings of lovers, the brotherly and sisterly af-fection of siblings and friends, and the divine love of God for us. In the English language, however, one word tries to convey all three of these meanings and all of the variations among the three meanings. We say, "I love my mom and dad. I love apple pie. I love my German Shepherd. I love Angela Bassett. I love gospel music. I love my wife!" Yet what we mean by the word love varies in each of those sentences.

As a matter of painful fact, one of the problems Dr. Thomas high-lights in these messages is what he calls a "fusion" of the four stages in relationships-romance, love, sex, and reproduction. A careful reading of this text demonstrates that what the author and the average reader mean when they use the word love in this paradigm has more to do with attraction than with a permanent and life-long commitment.

Love as it is understood by most people in terms of Dr. Thomas's paradigm has nothing to do with the covenantal commitment between two persons who offer themselves into God's hand for keeping "until death do us part." It only has to do with the Americanized notion of "falling in love" and "being in love."

That tragic and truncated understanding of love completely misses the mark in terms of understanding that "God is love" (1 John 4:16)! That misunderstanding also causes us to miss the mark in terms of living with the reality that genuine love means "I love you even when I do not feel like it."

Dr. Thomas wrestles with the cultural understanding of love that misleads most couples. He also argues for an a priori relationship with God as the prerequisite to any healthy understanding of being in a relationship with another human being.

This volume is must-read for all persons who are serious about making a commitment to God and making a commitment to another human being. I recommend it to teachers, to teenagers, and to believers of all ages.

Dr. Jeremiah A. Wright Jr.
Trinity United Church of Christ
Chicago, Illinois

Preface

It has been suggested by some people that we live in a culture of addiction. I have come to believe this assertion, based upon personal and pastoral experiences that have generated tremendous growth, maturity, and depth of thought in my life. I once thought that when one spoke of addiction, one was speaking exclusively of chemical and substance addiction (alcohol and drugs). Later, I was able to expand my understanding of addiction to include work, food, sex, caffeine, gambling, violence, exercise, computers, and so on. I even came to realize that it is possible to be addicted to other people. For example, some people are addicted to the substance abuser, who in turn is addicted to the drugs; or a pastor is addicted to the church, and the pastor's spouse in turn is addicted to the pastor. But all of this experience led to thinking about an addiction that seems to be more expansive than the ones I have mentioned. In fact, I believe the human family is heavily addicted to popular notions of love and romance. Love and romance are a legitimate part of human life, but our culture makes such exaggerated claims about the two that the pursuit of them becomes unhealthy at best and dangerous at worst. The exaggerated claims are summed up and expressed in the popular music and advertising mantras, *Love is all you need* and *Love is the answer*.

It is difficult to make a convincing assertion of addiction without a strict definition of the same. But to fully grasp my definition, we must locate addiction as a family illness. Some families rigidly believe that the addicted member of the family is the problem. If the particular addiction is alcohol, then the family identifies the alcoholic person (scapegoat) as the source of the family sickness. I have come to see that the drinking of the alcoholic is not the sole problem; rather, it is a symptom of a deeper family problem. Drinking is only one family member's response to the deeper family problem. Everyone in the family experiences the family problem, and there are probably many other unhealthy responses, but the response of the one alcoholic family member becomes the exclusive focus of the family. With all of this understood, we can define addiction as *any person, place, or thing that chronically takes one away from true relationship with the family.* In other words, addiction takes place when the person gives up on true relationship in a family and chronically substitutes a person, place, or thing for that which is perceived to be not possible in a family.

But we were made for true relationship within family. I believe that to a large extent, survival and self-esteem depend upon those among whom we are born—the family. Even if we are not among those who biologically birthed us, we learn to think, talk, read, and count—to be human—among some form of family. We learn to grow, mature, and discern what is lawful in the context of school family, church family, fraternity and sorority family. The family is a relational network that passes on truth, beliefs, values, patterns of behavior, and language. To the extent that these are healthy and mature, then there is true relationship in the family. But to the extent that they are unhealthy and immature, then the addictive cycles of behavior prevalent in the human family flourish.

By suggesting that we are addicted to love and romance, I am implying that popular notions of love and romance function to take us away from the family. We believe that these notions are bringing us closer to the family or that they form the basis of family, but in actuality the exaggerated claims become a substitute for family. Popular notions of love and romance take us away from the family by glossing over the harsh realities of human nature. Hence, notions of love and romance function as means of escape and denial for us.

I now introduce an idea that will become more and more evident throughout the pages of this book: the addiction to love and romance, and any other addiction, may be broken by the enlightened pursuit of spiritual values as a means of dealing with life's harsh realities. This devotional guide seeks to allow the Spirit of God to address life in all of its difficulties and to teach us to develop enlightened self-interest. All of this is addressed in the title, *What's Love Got to Do with It? Love, Power, Sex, and God.* What do the popular notions of love, romance, power, and sex have to do with real life as given by the Spirit of God? When real life is given by the Spirit of God, that life breaks the addictive cycles.

Pastor Frank Thomas
Mississippi Boulevard Christian Church
Memphis, Tennessee

Acknowledgments

A sermon is the collection of the thinking, living, and dreaming before God of many people, and not just the preacher alone. In many instances, the preacher is simply the channel or vehicle through which the Holy Spirit addresses the people of God through Scripture, and the people of God address the Scripture in dialogue with God. The essays contained herein, which were originally preached as sermons, are a reflective dialogue between God and the people around relationships, and the preacher is the mouthpiece for the discussion. I would like to thank many kind people for participating in the dialogue.

I would like to thank all of the people of New Faith Baptist Church, the place in which the original sermon series was conceived. I would like to thank the members of that congregation for the years they helped me to grow and develop as a preacher. This was some of my best preaching work among them.

I want to say thank you to all of the people who told me, as a pastor, their stories and experiences; who challenged me to keep my preaching real; who cried in my office; who told me deep secrets, many that had never been uttered before; who overcame unbelievable situations with bold steps of faith; who trusted me as their pastor; who believed that if I ever used their experience in a sermon that the names would be changed to protect the innocent.

I say thank you to my mother, the Reverend Dr. Almetha Thomas; my father, John Frank Thomas; my sister, the Reverend Angela Edwards; and my brother, Frederick Thomas, for the incubation that allowed me and my thinking to blossom and flower.

I want to say thanks to the Reverend Jini Kilgore Ross, whose kind introduction and simple question led to these sermons coming out of the files and back to life in such powerful ways. I never gave up on the dream that they would live again, but every dream needs a new spark for the flame every now and then. Thank you for igniting the flame.

I want to say thank you to my wife, Joyce Scott Thomas, who taught me what love had to do with it.

I want to say thank you to three of my key mentors, Dr. Henry Mitchell, Dr. Jeremiah A. Wright Jr., and Dr. Frederick G. Sampson III.

And I want to say thank you to the family of Mississippi Boulevard Christian Church in Memphis, Tennessee, for the opportunity to take this kind of preaching to another level.

Joyfully submitted,
Frank A. Thomas

Introduction

A fter she had listened to one of my sermons that addressed several of the issues of love and romance, I received a letter from a young lady. She wrote:

> It's interesting that you often talk about what has happened and where we go wrong, but I would like to hear more about Where do I go from here?

She raised a fascinating point that I had to agree with. Most of us preachers are much better at diagnosing the problem and analyzing what people have done or are doing wrong than we are at giving solutions that help people move forward to healing in their lives. Many preachers are experts at bad news but novices at concrete gospel solutions that give people hope. She was right; she deserved to hear more that might help her discern where she might go from here.

But how to move forward is a matter of the discernment of the will and purpose of God in one's life, which can be judged only in the depths of a person's individual relationship with God. Try as we might, preachers cannot go into the deepest areas of a person's one-on-one relationship with God, and therefore we are severely limited in telling people where to go from here. Preachers, parents, teachers, and others can coach—add interesting experience and thinking to one's life—but people must discern for themselves, through prayer and the reading of Scripture, where they go from here.

My job in these pages is to function as a coach—to give you, the reader, the benefit of careful thinking, prayer, and biblical truth. I do not purport to be right about everything. I am not trying to be right about everything. I am trying to be honest. I am trying to do honest reflection about real life and its intersection with a real gospel. I am shaping my thinking and beliefs in the attempt to help you shape your thinking and beliefs.

My contribution to your arrival at where you should go from here, or in discerning God's will in your life, includes a two-part process that I hope you as an individual, family, or study group will commit to. First, pray and read the entire Scripture text before reading each essay, and then answer the questions at the end of each chapter. If you will do these things, I believe that this book will be empowered to help you understand and break any addictive cycle that might be in your life. Too, I believe this book will help you discover God's will for your life.

Chapter One

The Nonpursuing Love of God

Luke 15:11-24, NIV

Jesus continued: "There was a man who had two sons. The younger one said to his father, 'Father, give me my share of the estate.' So he divided his property between them.

"Not long after that, the younger son got together all he had, set off for a distant country and there squandered his wealth in wild living. After he had spent everything, there was a severe famine in that whole country, and he began to be in need. So he went and hired himself out to a citizen of the country, who sent him to his fields to feed pigs. He longed to fill his stomach with the pods that the pigs were eating, but no one gave him anything.

"When he came to his senses, he said, 'How many of my father's hired men have food to spare, and here I am starving to death! I will set out and go back to my father and say to him: 'Father, I have sinned against heaven and against you. I am no longer worthy to be called your son; make me like one of your hired men.' So he got up and went to his father.

"But while he was still a long way off, his father saw him and was filled with compassion for him; he ran to his son, threw his arms around him and kissed him.

"The son said to him, 'Father, I have sinned against heaven and against you. I am no longer worthy to be called your son.'

"But the father said to the servants, 'Quick! Bring the best robe and put it on him. Put a ring on his finger and sandals on his feet. Bring the fattened calf and kill it. Let's have a feast and celebrate. For this son of mine was dead and is alive again; he was lost and is found.' So they began to celebrate."

What comes to mind when you think about addiction in families? Usually, when people talk about addiction, they are speaking about substance abuse and chemical dependency. When their understanding of addiction enlarges, they discover that one can be addicted to food, to work, to gambling, to sex, to caffeine, to tobacco, to violence, to exercise, and even to people. I once heard someone admit in a moment of enlightened self-awareness, "He is addicted to drugs, and I am addicted to him." But there is another form of addiction that I believe is number one in our country and world today: the addiction to love and romance. The exploration of the addiction to love and romance has prompted this collection of messages. Throughout this volume I propose to you, the reader, that the addiction to love and romance is more prevalent than the addictions to food, work, sex, or even drugs and alcohol. The addiction to love and romance is the most pervasive addiction in the world.

What is an addiction? An addiction is any person, place, or thing that chronically takes one away from relationship with the family. Work can chronically take one away from relationship with the family. Food can chronically take one away from relationship with the family. Drugs can chronically take one away from relationship with the family. Anything that takes one away from relationship with the family is a substitute for relationship with the family. Addiction is a substitute for relationship with the family. Believing that relationship is not available to us, we go to substitutes: work, food, tobacco, caffeine, sex, drugs, alcohol, exercise, computers, television, and cars. It is paradoxical: we become addicted to love and romance seeking relationship, but our addiction takes us away from the true relationship we seek.

Many of us are looking for a relationship that will take away our pain. Many of us are looking for relationships that will help us stop hurting. We think that love will take our pain away. We think to ourselves, "If I could just get love. If I could just find the right one and fall in love"; hence, the tremendous addiction to love and romance. We want to believe that there is some woman or some man who will give us the love that we need, and we will live happily ever after. We want to believe, as Tammy Terrell and Marvin Gaye sang, that there "ain't no mountain high enough; ain't no valley low enough to keep me from gettin' to you, babe." If I could just get to you, everything would be all right. We believe that love and being in love with love will take all of our pain away. If we can just love, it will be all right.

The Broadway hit song "And I'm Telling You I'm Not Going" is a classic example of the addiction to love and romance that I am talking about. Jennifer Holliday declares in that song:

> I ain't never met no man like you. And I can't even imagine my life without you. I can't live without you. I just can't live without you. You're gonna love me. You're gonna love me. I don't wanna be free. You're gonna love me.[1]

What kind of foolishness is that? You're going to *make* somebody love you? How are you going to *make* someone love you? "I can't live without you." Well, why can't she live without him? She cannot live without him because she is using him to try to keep from dealing with a fundamental reality in life: that life is a painful thing. No diva, no man, no singing group, no relationship is going to make life stop hurting. We use love and romance as a substitute for relationship, believing that love and romance will stop the pain. But what does love have to do with it? What does love have to do with taking the pain away?

What about a kind of love that will help us to face all of our pain rather than take it away? We need relationships like that. We need relationships that will help us to recognize that we are not whole and that will assist us in the struggle to become whole. No matter what you do, you can't get around the basic fact that life is painful and that it must be lived on its own terms. There is no woman, there is no man, there are no material things, there is no sex that will make life stop hurting. *Life will hurt, so you have one of two choices: try to escape the hurt and discover an addiction, or try to face the hurt and grow from it.* Those are the only two choices you have. Either you can continue to find escapes that will ultimately become addictive, or you can face life for what it is and grow up.

A real relationship helps us to face the truth that life is a hurting thing, but even a relationship cannot take away pain. Relationships can only help us to face the pain or help us to escape from it. Not even a relationship with the church will take away one's pain. The truth of the matter is that God will not take away our pain, and our relationship with God will either help us to face the pain and deal with and grow from it, or it will help us to escape it. For people can use God, church, Scriptures, prayer, and worship services as escapes from reality (substitutes) or as agencies of courage to confront reality. Such agencies of courage permit people to deal with, grow from, and be victorious over reality.

Most of us want to deny, overcome, or get rid of our pain as soon as possible, but that is not always such a good idea because we do not grow to live our best lives without working through our pain. Even if God were to explain to us in person the best way to live, we would probably say, "Yeah, God, you're right. We're going to do that." But most of us will not do it because *unmotivated people are invulnerable to insight,*[2] *which means that people who are not motivated to change don't hear insights.* So God comes along and by the power of the Holy Spirit shares insight about what real living is and how we can have real fulfillment in living, but because we are unmotivated to change, we are invulnerable to insight. The question is not whether the insight has been shared; the question is Do you have ears to hear? But most of us are not motivated until we become tired of hurting. When we get sick and tired of the pain, we become available for insight. If we remove the pain too quickly, then we lose all motivation to change. Pain is the prime human motive for change, and we must ask the question when we rescue people from their pain, Are we helping them? God will help us. God will leave us in the pain and confront us with the choice to grow or to become addicted. God will allow us the freedom of our choice.

There are people who will not allow us the freedom of our own choice. There are people who rescue us from our pain and the freedom of choice. These people are called *enablers*. Enablers are people who try to stop other people from having to face the fact that life is a painful thing. Enablers are people who try to fix the pain of other people. People who try to keep people from facing the consequences of their behavior are enablers. Enablers are people who help others avoid a fundamental lesson of living, which is that pain forces us to change.

A boy gets in trouble, and the family is concerned about its name, status, and position. The boy is down at the police station, so mom and daddy jump up in the middle of the night and run down there to try to fix it, to prevent the boy from having to bear the consequences of his action, and to preserve the family name in the community. The sickness in this boy will probably continue because the parents are enabling it. When are we going to realize that nobody has a great family? What family name are we trying to protect? Every family I know is basically dysfunctional, and praise God that it is not possible for us to act out all the dysfunctions that are in our families. In other words, despite what we grew up in, some of us are amazingly healthy.

A spouse calls to tell the boss that the husband is sick when the truth is that he is drunk. The boss has said if the husband misses one more day, he will be fired. So the mama looks across the room and sees two kids and the drunken daddy. The mama knows that the income is needed, so she gets on the phone and begs the boss, even offering to come in herself. That is an example of enabling. I understand that some of us are living with some difficult choices. We are trying to raise the kids, so we make some difficult decisions, but we need to look at our problems from a long-term perspective. Yes, I understand that the spouse is trying to save her husband's job so the kids can eat, but I am saying that she had better start looking at her long-term situation. The truth is that if she saves his job once, she will save it fifty times. The long-term prospects in a such situation are not that bright because if a person chooses drugs or alcohol over his or her family, then one might want to think about what the future will be like with this spouse.

To the degree that we try to fix the pain of others, we become the disease. We are the sickness, and we will make others sick. Some of the most vicious enabling goes on in the church under the guise of helping people. Often members of the church call the church for help on behalf of their friends and relatives. Usually someone's rent is unpaid, or food is scarce, or the bills are overdue. When church officers research the situation they often find that there is an addictive cycle of drugs and alcohol, so the church will not pay the rent. The officers will say to the family, "We can offer you some helpful resources, but cash is not available."

Then the member who made the referral angrily calls and says, "I thought y'all supposed to be helping people." Well, we are helping people, but we are not *enabling* people. Our mission is to assist people with their one-on-one relationship with God. The word *assist* is chosen carefully. The church is not their relationship with God. The church is a place that assists them with their one-on-one relationship with God. When one quits on God because church members are not acting the way one thinks they should act, that one is missing the point. The church and the pastor are there to assist. If the church and the pastor are not functioning the way one thinks they ought to be functioning, that's all right. The church is offering only a little bit of assistance, anyway. *Each person is primarily responsible for his or her one-on-one relationship with God.* If the church votes to purchase pink and purple choir robes and somebody doesn't think she looks good in pink and purple, she would do well not to become overinvested in choir robes and leave the church. People in the church are to assist, not to enable.

Many people want the church to enable them. Many want the church to take away their pain, so we have an ideal picture of a perfect church where everybody loves everybody; we all sit around campfires and sing "Kumbaya" and have good feelings. And what we're talking about is good feelings because we think that good feelings help us heal. But do good feelings help us to grow up? Sometimes we function better when we feel bad. *We have to learn to separate function from feeling.* We might be feeling bad, but the church functions better than it ever has. We might be feeling good, but the place is sick as can be.

What kind of love helps us to face our pain? I call it nonpursuing love. How about a love that allows us to face our pain until we decide to grow from our hurt? How about a love that backs off and allows us to hurt until we decide to grow from our hurt? How about a love that does not rescue? How about a love that does not pursue? Let's look at the love of the father in the story of the prodigal son.

In the story of the prodigal son, the boy goes to his father and says, "Give me my money. I know you're loaded. I've been living here a long time now. I've seen it. I don't know how much, but I know you got some, so fork it over. It's mine." Then he decides to go to the far country and live riotously, as the Bible says. He becomes a party favorite and man about town. He shows up in a limo. He leaves in a limo. He has a high-rise apartment overlooking the river. He is living large and loud. He brings his friends over for a little party; then they go to the afterparty and sit in the booth at the back of the club and check out the ladies. He's living fast, and fast living is what it is—fast living.

But all of a sudden, it goes out faster than it comes in, and it begins to slip. The limo bill comes, and he can't pay it; the tab at the back of the club where he checked out the ladies comes due, and he can't pay it, so the club tells him no more tabs. The rent becomes due on his high-rise apartment, and he doesn't have it, so the manager asks him to move. The son slowly begins to descend. He comes down to the level where he has to take a job, and not only a job but any job. A job for a Jewish boy slopping slop for pigs is low. That's the lowest of the low. He slops for pigs, and as he's throwing slop around, he remembers his daddy, and he says, "The servants in my daddy's house make more than this." And he's humble enough to say, "I'll go to my daddy and ask him if I can have a servant's job."

Much of the focus of the story is always on the son. Traditionally, the way we interpret this is with the daddy on the porch, looking for his son every day. The daddy is worried about his son every day. The daddy cannot go on with his life and wipes a tear from his eye every day when he thinks about his son out there somewehere. The daddy goes out to the porch every day and looks up to the road to see if his son is on his way home. Well, I don't see that perspective in the story.

Let's look at the daddy. How does the daddy function? Let's assume that the daddy knew the boy, which means the daddy knew that he was probably going to waste the money. A lot of us would have given the boy the check, then thought about it later and called the bank to stop payment. A lot of us would have figured how to ration the money. We would have sent a hundred dollars a week. But the Bible says the daddy gave the boy the money. The daddy knew in all probability that the boy was going to squander the money, but the daddy still believed that the boy knew how to run his life, and if he did not, this was the path that the boy needed to take to learn how to manage his life.

The Father Assumed the Boy Knew How to Run His Life

The father's assumption is radical because many times when we think about our children or important people in our lives, we think that they do not know how to run their lives, and we assume that they do not know what they are doing. As soon as we make that assumption, we move into a rescuing position. Our rescuing position registers as a vote of no confidence in our loved one. The father's position is radical because it assumes that his son knows how to run his life without the father's fixing, explaining, maneuvering, or manipulating on his behalf.

The Son's Decisions Did Not Change the Father's Love

Second, the relationship with the boy was not dependent on the boy's plan to run his life. I believe that when the boy ran out of money, he called home to be rescued by his dad. He called home and asked for more money. I believe the father would not send him anything. The father took no more responsibility than what was legitimately his. The boy made his bed, and the boy was going to have to lie in it. The daddy stayed in contact with the boy, but he did not rescue or pursue the boy. He did not agree with the boy's choices or decisions, but that does not mean that he and his boy could not remain in deep relationship. The father stayed in contact with the boy regardless of whether or not he agreed with the boy's decisions and how the boy chose to run his life. When the boy asked for more money, the father could say no. It is possible to say no and remain in contact with people who are important to us. I like to think the father said, "No, I am not going to send you any money, but I will call you next week."

The Father Let the Boy Hurt

Third, the father let the boy hurt. A lot of us are like hurt police. As soon as people who are important to us are on the verge of any kind of hurt, we run in and flash our badge. Hurt Police. As soon as our kids have to go through something, as soon as our spouse has to go through something, as soon as somebody has to go through something, we flash our badge: Hurt Police. We think our job is to block any hurt coming into a person's life. The father knew the boy was in trouble, but the father let the boy hurt. The father understood that hurt heals. We think that hurt policing is protecting our children. The father knew that he could not protect his son from real life.

The Father Avoided I-Told-You-So Love

Fourth, when the son came home, the father did not have what I call "I-told-you-so love." Do you know what I-told-you-so love is? It is rescuing advice based upon the rescuer's prediction of the outcome of another person's anticipated action. When the prediction comes true, the rescuer says, "I told you so," which has the effect of rubbing salt in the wound. It has the effect of proving and establishing the wisdom and competency of the person offering the advice and not of building up the resources of the one who has to deal with a less than desirable outcome. I-told-you-so love hurts. It sounds like this:

"I *told* you that she was from the wrong side of the tracks."
"I *told* you their mama wasn't nothin'."
"I *told* you. You could have saved yourself and me."
"I *told* you that he wasn't much. I knew it. I just knew it. I couldn't put my finger on it. I couldn't name it, but it just didn't seem right. I just knew it. I *told* you."

The daddy didn't say, " I told you." I believe the daddy was going on with his life. The daddy had invested and received enough return to more than compensate for what he had given the son. The Bible says he looked up the road and saw the son coming, and he ran up the road and hugged his son. Nowhere in that text does it say, "I told you so."

Love for the Son Did Not Destroy the Father

Fifth, the daddy did not allow his love for his son to become self-destructive. Have you ever said that mama would be alive today if she had not worried so about her wayward children? Do you know that there are some parents who allow their children to worry them to death? And such love occurs not only between parents and children but also between pastors and churches, brothers and sisters, friends and friends. I have seen a fine, beautiful, and upstanding woman be dragged down into the gutter by a trifling and a no-good man, and she claims that she is in love. She was a princess who gave up the whole kingdom to come down and marry this peasant. You do not let anybody drag you down to the gutter. If a child goes away to school and flunks out because he or she is partying and playing bid whist instead of studying, and the family has taken its savings to try to pay the tuition but the child decides to try to go to another school and asks the family to pay for it, the family's response ought to be, "Maybe you should get a job and earn this degree on your own." We call bailing out the child love. Are the parents supposed to lose all of their savings behind a child who will not be responsible? Some of us have the audacity to call this love. What does love have to do with it?

In our text the father says, "My son who was dead." That means the father had already had a funeral and grieved and gone on with his life. Why are you going to let your children worry you to the grave? Why are you going to let your spouse worry you into high blood pressure, heart disease, or stroke? Some of these folk are dead. But look at the joy of the father when he discovers his son coming up the road. It was not befitting for a Jewish father to run. But he rejoiced because his son, who was dead, was now alive. His son, who was lost, was now found. Go on with your lives. If your spouse walks out because he or she is following a plan for his or her own life, go on with your life. Grieve and have a funeral. Do your grief work, and go on with your life. If you have a substance-abusing spouse, go on with your life. Love does not mean that you have to give up your life, that you have to give up your happiness in the name of love. That is not love. That is addiction. That is a substitute for a relationship. The daddy did not allow his love for his son to become self-destructive.

We need to face the pain, the very real pain of this life, but it is impossible to face the pain and the addiction that it leads to without Christ. It is not possible to face life for what life really is, with all of its pain and disappointment, without Christ. If we do not have Christ, we succumb to addictions. We surrender to drugs. We surrender to our work. We have to "fall in love." We need Christ. There is no other way. You can get a big title and a big position making lots of money. You can be popular and famous. Sooner or later you will discover the nature of addictions and that you need Christ.

For its fiftieth-year anniversary issue, *Sports Illustrated* chose Muhammad Ali as the sportsman of its first fifty years. During the interview Ali said, and I paraphrase, "I've had fortune. I've had power. I've had the whole thing, and I just want to say one thing." The interviewer said that, almost whispering, Ali said, "It ain't nothing."

Christ is the only one who will move you from addiction to true relationship. Christ is the only one. I could not even begin to live without addictions if I did not have Christ.

---

[1] Henry Krieger and Tom Eyen, "And I'm Telling You I'm Not Going," ASCAP (Dreamgirls Music) and BMI.

[2] Dr. Edwin Friedman in lectures in Bethesda, Maryland.

Study Questions

1. In "The Nonpursuing Love of God" Dr. Thomas introduces a major premise of the book: that many people are addicted to relationships in an attempt to alleviate the pain that is a part of life. How can one distinguish real love from relationship addiction?

2. Why does Dr. Thomas assert that even church and God, Scriptures and prayer, can be addictive escapes from reality instead of redeeming agencies of courage?

3. What are some things enablers can do to stop being hurt police?

4. Give an example of a situation that was helped when someone was forced to face the pain and grow from the hurt.

5. Look at the chapter subheadings below that describe the father's attitude toward his prodigal son. Give examples for each subheading from the Bible, history, contemporary life, or personal experience.
   - The father assumed the boy knew how to run his life
   - The son's decisions did not change the father's love (nor did the father try to change the son's mind)
   - The father let the boy hurt
   - The father avoided I-told-you-so love
   - Love for the son did not destroy the father

Prayer Thought: I will seek to love others in a way that preserves both my integrity and theirs.

Chapter Two

The Greatest Power on Earth

John 10:17-18, NASB

"For this reason the Father loves Me, because I lay down My life that I may take it again. No one has taken it away from me, but I lay it down on My own initiative. I have authority to lay it down, and I have authority to take it up again. This commandment I received from My Father."

So many people feel that they have so little real power. They seem to feel that they are powerless within the relationships and the institutions that are critical to their lives. Many people perceive themselves to have virtually no power on their jobs, virtually no power with the government, and virtually no power in their church, and virtually no power at home. Many people experience themselves as powerless.

I know of women who think that men have all the power. I know of men who think that women have all the power. There are some black people who think white people have the power, and some white people who think black people have the power. Some of the clergy think laypeople have the power, and some laypeople think the clergy have the power. We can say there is a tremendous sense of powerlessness in our culture today. Well, who does have the power, and what is power?

When we talk about power, we typically talk about it in the world's terms, which define it as authority over people. Power in this sense is the ability to make people do what you want them to do even when they do not want to do it. Another worldly view is financial power, which some consider to be the greatest power in the world: the power to buy goods and services, the power to go where one wants to go and spend what one wants to spend. Financial power confers the ability for some people to worry only about whether they want something and not to worry about the price. For others the greatest power on earth is found in guns, bombs, and missiles. Such persons believe that whoever has the biggest weapon and the most bombs and bullets will ultimately win.

I, however, am foolish enough to suggest that the most awesome power is the power within yourself. What I want to suggest is that the greatest power on earth is the power that comes from God to manage our own lives and maximize our own futures and God-given destinies. In other words, the greatest power on earth is the God-given authority to be who God made us to be. The greatest power on earth is the power to be one's self. The greatest power on earth is the power to maximize one's future and to live one's destiny. Jesus lives out of that power when he says, "Nobody takes my life from me, but I lay it down of my own accord. It is my own decision. I lay my life down when I want to, and I pick it up when I get ready. I have this command from my Father. This is my life. Nobody takes it. I have power and authority over my own life. This I have received from my Father." In this paraphrase of Jesus' words, Jesus is speaking out of his full authority to be what God created him to be.

What is so particularly bothersome to me about much of what I see going on in our culture, especially in relationships, is that people are giving huge amounts of their personal power away to other people. What I see is a whole lot of powerful people who have given their power away and who, in their thinking, experience themselves as powerless. Yet, no one is powerless. We are all tremendously powerful people; we simply have some among us who may not be aware that they have given all their power away. God made us powerful. God made us awesome. The question is whether we exercise and own the power that we have. Or do we irresponsibly give it away?

We have a glorious name for the giving away of our personal power. Many of us call it love. I see it every day in our culture. Some man or some woman gives away all of his or her personal power in the name of love. She gives her body; he gives his career. She gives her job; he gives his life, all in the name of love. The persons to whom they give their power abuse it because they are not supposed to have it in the first place. When people get what they are not supposed to have, they usually do not know what to do with it, so they abuse it, and after they abuse it, many of us sit around and sing sad songs about being victims of love.

This victim-of-love thinking is all over our culture. A song from the African American woman's classic *Waiting to Exhale* speaks to this victim-of-love thinking. It says, "I'm not gonna cry, I'm not gonna cry / I ain't gonna shed no tear." One line in particular stopped me: "I woulda stopped breathing if you had told me to."[1] And I said, "Wait, wait, wait, wait, wait! 'I would have stopped breathing if you had told me to.' " Breathing is essential. Breathing is God-given. She would have interrupted God's plan for her existence if he had told her to? What makes her give away all of her power? The general theme of the song is that she has given up her career and dreams to help his career and dreams, and in the face of her sacrifice he has the audacity to leave her now that his career has taken off. In her pain and anguish she complains, "I was your secretary and should have left you a long time ago." She is right. She should have left him a long time ago. What is she doing, taking care of some grown man and not getting equal return out of the relationship?

What is in her life that makes her stay with him and take unequal treatment? What about her life? What about her career? What about her purpose? What about her dreams? What about her destiny? What about her soul? We don't want to talk about that. We want to sit around and sing sad songs and play the victim. We want to sit around and talk about being a prisoner of love. But what does love have to do with it? That is what I want to know. What does love have to do with giving away one's personal power? Why does she think anybody is going to care about her life if she does not care about it?

Our parents are the only ones who are going to take care of us, if anybody, so why do we think that people are going to give us equal return in relationships if we do not expect it and demand it? What does love have to do with it? We are talking about power, but a lot of us use love to keep from dealing with issues of power in relationships. What does love have to do with it?

We have come to equate love with giving our personal power away, and we read this interpretation into the text. This text is at the heart of what is known as the Good Shepherd Discourse (John 10:1-21). In it, Jesus speaks about his relationship with the church, using shepherding as an analogy. Jesus draws a distinction between the bad shepherd, who is a thief and a robber, and the good shepherd. The sheep will not listen to the thief and the robber because they are intimately attuned to the good shepherd's voice. The thief has come only to steal, kill, and destroy, but the good shepherd has come that they might have life and have it more abundantly. When danger is present, the good shepherd lays down his life for the sheep while the thief and the robber run away to protect themselves. God loves the good shepherd because he lays down his life for the sheep. Jesus is the good shepherd because he lays down his life for the sheep.

If we are not careful, we will read this laying down of one's life for the sheep as giving up self and giving away personal power. If we are not careful, we will read this passage as justification for the kind of love that functions as a total ignoring of one's self and that supports one's need to help others. If we are not careful, the self-sacrificing love of this text will become justification for being a doormat, or giving sex, or allowing ourselves to have our esteem assaulted, allowing ourselves to be physically and verbally abused, allowing ourselves to be two-timed, allowing ourselves to be stuck with a bunch of babies, all under the pretense that we are in love with somebody.

But what does love have to do with being two-timed? What does love have to do with giving sex? What does love have to do with allowing one's self-esteem to be assaulted? What does love have to do with being physically and verbally abused? One of the real issues in a relationship is the distribution of power and how both parties feel about the distribution. I believe the overexaggeration of love and romance functions to distract the parties from issues of power. Rather than talk about power distribution, we talk about the illusion of love.

The problem is, you cannot love anybody if you do not have a self. Love can be love only if the one who is exercising love has a self. Love is love only if you keep your personal power. You see, love and power are connected. You do not give up all your power and call that love. You do not become a doormat and call that love. Real love allows for personal power. Real love enhances, builds, and develops personal power. As a matter of fact, love is built on the base of personal power.

For some reason, whenever you start talking about having a self, someone gets nervous and says you are being *selfish*. I am not talking about being selfish; I am talking about having a self. We live under the illusion that the way to have goodness in the world is to not have a self, to sacrifice one's self. To give up one's self, to lose one's self. But in this text, Jesus exercises love in the context of self. When Jesus says, "Nobody takes my life; I lay it down, and I pick it up when I get ready," he is talking about love within the context of a self. He is clear that he owns his life and has made the choice to sacrifice. Even though he is laying down his life, he keeps and maintains his personal power. This is the value of the statement "I pick it up when I get ready." Jesus gives up his life and reserves his life at the same time.

Jesus is clear. I lay my life down of my will, my accord, my decision. I have the authority to manage and direct my life. I can lay it down and pick it back up again. Nobody takes my life; I am not a victim. I offer my life of my free will. Rather than exercise our power in this manner, we use the language of love to camouflage our abuse of power. Consequently, we lose sight of the God-given power that emanates from our individuality with all of its hopes, dreams, uniqueness, and choice, and we deem ourselves to be powerless.

If we are called to sacrifice, we must sacrifice on the basis of a self.

17

Addiction, not love, sacrifices all of one's personal power because there is no sense of self. True sacrifice is based on a sense of self. Self-sacrificing love is a biblically valid model for operation in relationships, but when it is based on non self, it is destructive.

In *I Asked for Intimacy,* Renita Weems explains the destructive power of non-self-love in women who are relationship addicts. She writes,

> Relationship addiction is why some women have settled for a married man. Relationship addiction is why the mother pretended not to notice that the father was leaving her bedroom in the middle of the night for the daughter's. Relationship addiction is why, despite warnings, the employee has started to take long coffee breaks with the biggest flirt in the office. Relationship addiction is why the woman didn't say anything last night when the man didn't put on the condom that she had placed on the night table.[2]

What is going on in your life that you would allow some of these situations? What is going on in your life that you do not exercise your personal power? What is going on that you demote your God-given authority and give it to somebody else who has no business having it, and so when he abuses it you want to come to church and sing sad songs and ask God to do something about the situation when you ain't gonna do nothing about it?

Relationship addiction is why you have settled for a married man. Relationship addiction is why your mother pretended not to notice while your father was leaving her bedroom in the middle of the night for yours. Relationship addiction is why you didn't say anything last night when he didn't put on the condom you placed on the night table. You need to know that *you can keep your personal power and still love somebody.* Yes, you can.

Remember, the challenge of relationship is how to be close and still preserve a self. Remember, anybody can fall in love and give away self, but the challenge is to fall in love and still preserve a self. The challenge is how to get close to people but still be you. So we have a dynamic tension: we need people in our lives, for if we get out too far, we will not have relationships and we will not grow, but if we get in too close, we lose ourselves. Our job is to find the right distance where we can love somebody yet preserve self. We are looking for a space that is close but still permits us to have a self, a space where we can be in relationship but still have a self. We can be in love but still have a self!

We find in this tenth chapter of John that Jesus is talking about love as a choice. We talk about love as an emotion. Jesus talks about love as a decision. We talk about love as a feeling. Jesus talks about love as an act of the will. We talk about love at the tip of Cupid's arrow. We talk about love as a kind of homey togetherness in which we think the same way, feel the same way, look the same way, dress the same way, and talk the same way. It is the same, and we are in love because we both like the same things and have much in common. We both went to the same school, and we are from the same socioeconomic background. But you can think differently and still be in love. You can have a different career plan and still be in love. You can be members of different churches and still be in love. You can be different and still be in love. You don't have to give up your self to be in love.

We are talking about love as romance. Jesus is talking about love as the power to maximize one's future and live one's God-given destiny. Jesus is talking about the possibility of having some distance and space between one another yet still being in love. Jesus is talking about sharing some of your personal power with people but taking it back if they do not know what to do with it. Didn't he tell his disciples that if their word was rejected by the people in a house or a city, to shake the dust off of their feet and move on (Matthew 10:14)? Jesus is talking about love as a choice that we extend to people, but we are talking about love as an addiction to take away all of our pain. Jesus is talking about love that is on top of a base of a self, but we are talking about the hungering for a relationship and love because we do not have a self.

The field of science provides a useful analogy between the immune system and the ability to have a self. Scientists have learned that individuals must have an immune system in order to touch others. They say the function of the immune system is not only to fight off diseases but also to preserve the integrity of the organism. Therefore, you and I could not touch if we did not have an immune system because without an immune system we would just become a glob and lose the integrity of ourselves. A scientific experiment was performed in which the immune system was taken out of an organism. That organism was placed in a container with another organism that had an immune system, and they began to move toward one another. When the organism that had an immune system moved close to the organism that did not have an immune system, autodestruct was activated almost immediately within the organism without the immune system. It globbed and was swallowed up by the organism that had a system.

This is like a woman with very little sense of self who enters a relationship with a man. She moves toward him and he toward her, and when they are close, autodestruct activates in her, and she does not know who she is, or where she's going, or what she is doing, so she becomes depressed. And no, this does not happen just to women because there are men who do not have a self either, who get hooked on alcohol and drugs that induce autodestruct, so that they lose themselves. Some men are hooked on sex and bodies because something is missing down deep inside, so when they get close to a body, autodestruct activates, and they do not know who they are, they do not recall that they have commitments at home, they do not remember that they bowed down before God, so they do something that they have no business doing.

If you do not have an immune system, you cannot touch anybody. If you do not have a self, then do not touch anybody. If you do not have a self, do not go out with anybody. If you do not have a self, do not hang around with anybody. If you are lonely, stay home, because if your immune system has been compromised, then you are getting ready to get into a world of trouble. If you need to go out, stay home. If you go out when you do not need to go out, you will discover that you are better able to handle that which comes your way. It might be that you have to wait for your immune system to be intact before you venture out. When you do go out, you need to go as wise as a serpent (Matthew 10:16), looking for everything, suspecting everything, and not allowing anybody to catch you with your defenses (immune system) down. But we do not want to talk about that because we want to talk about being addicted to love. We want to talk about being taken advantage of. I am talking about what you can do to maintain your self.

If you do not have a self, then you had better be careful of touching people. You need to be like a man who, because his immune system was so compromised, could not catch germs and still live, so he had to live in a plastic bubble. If you do not have a self, maybe you need to put yourself in God's bubble until you develop a self. Maybe it is a good thing not to have anybody. Maybe it is a good thing to be by yourself until you develop a self. You see, if you do not have a self, you will become a glob and lose all principles of your organization. And losing all principles of your organization, you will not know who you are. When you forget who you are, you will hang around with anybody, and you will do anything. You will discover that you have lost your power.

Know That God Loves You

How do you develop a self? How do you acquire an immune system? First, you must know that God loves you. If your husband walks away, you must know that God loves you. If my church fires me, God loves me. If they give you a pink slip on your job, God loves you. If you get cancer, God loves you. You have to know way down, deep down, sho'nuff down that God loves you. God loves you. In verse 17, Jesus makes it clear that God loves him. He says, "The reason God loves me is that I lay down my life that I may take it again." Jesus is absolutely certain and clear that God loves him. This certainty is at the base of his self-actualizing personal power.

To know God's love, you must have an intimate and personal relationship with God. You cannot know God loves you if you come to church only once a month, or if you are irregular at choir rehearsal, or if you never show up for Bible class. God loves you, but you cannot get to prayer meeting? If you know God intimately and how wonderful the love of God is for you, then that love makes some radical changes in your life. Your sense of self will start with the fact that God loves you.

Know That God Gave You a Self

Second, you must know that God gave you a self. God gave you an identity. God gave you a uniqueness. God gave you an immune system. God gave you dreams. God gave you hopes. God gave life to you. Jesus said, "Nobody takes my life. I lay it down when I want to." My life. I like that. My life. Why are we so scared to say "my life"? This is my life. No, you cannot have it. This is mine. It is mine. I do what God tells me with my life. This is my life. My life. These are my hopes and my dreams. Mine. Mine. Mine.

I can share yours. I can participate with you in yours, and you in mine, but I've got to have mine. If I do not have mine, I cannot participate with you in yours. I cannot give up all of mine to help you in yours. My life. My hopes. Mine, mine, mine. Why are we so scared to say *mine?* We are worried about being misinterpreted and being selfish. But it is possible to say *mine* and still love. What I am saying is that we were like little souls up in heaven with little parachutes on our backs, and when the fullness of time came, God shoved us over the balcony of heaven with our little parachutes on and we fell through eternity, down through space, all the way to earth where we landed in our mamas' fallopian tubes. In other words, you are not an accident. God had you planned. God gave you a little nudge out of heaven. God had a purpose and a plan. Your mama and daddy may have been surprised, but God had you planned, which means you have a uniqueness. You have a purpose, an identity, and a calling. You have a reason for being. You might not know it, but you still have it. Nobody takes my purpose away, Jesus said. I lay it down when I want to.

Have a Vision for Your Life

Third, you must have a vision for your life. In other words, if you do not know where you want to be in five years, you are not going to get out of your present situation. If you do not have an agenda, people will write you into their program. And people who write you into their program can write you out of their program. If you have an agenda, however, you will be able to make a decision as to whether or not you will be written into anybody else's program.

What is your agenda? Where are you going? Where are you headed? What are you trying to accomplish? What are you trying to do? What is most important? What are your hopes? What are your dreams? We do not want to talk about all that. Instead, we want to play victim.

You see, when Jesus said, "I am going to lay my life down and pick it up when I get ready," that implied a plan. He was on his way somewhere. He understood. He did not just climb on the cross and say, "Oh, I was surprised this happened to me. Here I tried to heal all these people, and all they did was kick me in the teeth and put me up on the cross" (victim). The Bible says the Lamb of God was slain before the foundation of the world, which implies that before the world was formed, he had already died, which means that God understood that we were sinners. It means that God understood that Jesus would have to sacrifice for redemption before Adam and Eve, before the Garden, before the Lord Jesus said, "I will go." This is why he can say, "Nobody takes my life. It is already gone. The religious leaders do not take my life. It is already gone. The scribes, Pharisees, Pilate, the Sanhedrin, Caiaphas, Barabbas, Judas, and even Peter and all the other disciples do not take my life. Before the worlds were formed, it was already gone." Jesus had a vision, and love was a choice and not a necessity. When you acquire a vision, relationships are choices and not necessities.

23

If you have not found out how gifted you are, you are in for a nice surprise. If you do not know how talented you are, how awesome you are, how wonderful you are, how beautiful you are, how gifted, and if you do not know how much personal power you have, you are in for a nice surprise. All you've got to do is get in a relationship with God because when you get in a relationship with God, all kinds of nice surprises begin to happen. Go to some Bible studies and see what God will begin to do in your life. If you do not know how awesome you are, if you experience yourself as powerless, get in some prayer meetings and see what God will do with your life.

I say this because the God that I serve specializes. God specializes in putting immune systems back intact. If your immune system has been compromised, God knows how to restore it. God knows how to put broken lives back together. God knows how to put broken souls back together. God knows how to put broken people back together. God knows how to put broken dreams back together. God knows how to raise up your immune system. I do not care what you have done. I do not care how many mistakes you have made. I do not care how many boyfriends you have had. I do not care how many relationship mistakes you have made. I do not care that you are divorced. I do not care that you have had an affair. I do not care that you are addicted. I do not care that you've got cocaine on the brain. I do not care that you have messed up. The God that I serve specializes. The God that I serve puts folk back together. Broken lives come back together. The God that I serve is able to do it. God can put broken people back together. God can do it. Don't tell me about your past. Let me in on your future. Don't tell me about who did what to you. I want to know what you are going to do for yourself. I want to know if you are going to get in relationship with God and develop your self.

---

[1] Babyface, "Not Gon' Cry," BMI.

[2] Renita Weems, *I Asked for Intimacy: Stories of Blessing, Betrayal, and Birthings* (Philadephia: Innisfree Press, 1993).

Study Questions

1. Dr. Thomas says that the greatest power on earth is the power to be one's self. Using Jesus' words in John 10:17-18, Dr. Thomas shows that the one who came to set an example of the fulfilled life was concerned with the prerogative of personal power. In what ways do we give away our personal power? How can we retrieve it?

2. Why do we give away our personal power?

3. Among adults, are there any legitimate victims of love, or are so-called victims persons who have made bad decisions for themselves and relinquished their personal power?

4. Jesus said that the good shepherd lays down his life for the sheep and that there is no greater love than to give up one's life for another. Jesus urges us to sacrifice for others. How is this different from giving up personal power?

5. Jesus, says Dr. Thomas, talks about love as a choice, not an emotion. Can you give an example of love as an emotion? As a choice?

6. Develop a personal testimony for each of the subheading points in this chapter:
   • Know that God loves you
   • Know that God gave you a self
   • Have a vision for your life

Prayer Thought: I will share the gift of my self with others, but I will not give my self to anyone's keeping but God's.

Chapter Three

Stuck on Stupid

Ruth 1:11-18, NIV

But Naomi said, "Return home, my daughters. Why would you come with me? Am I going to have any more sons, who could become your husbands? Return home, my daughters; I am too old to have another husband. Even if I thought there was still hope for me—even if I had a husband tonight and then gave birth to sons—would you wait until they grew up? Would you remain unmarried for them? No, my daughters. It is more bitter for me than for you, because the Lord's hand has gone out against me!"

At this they wept again. Then Orpah kissed her mother-in-law good-by, but Ruth clung to her.

"Look," said Naomi, "your sister-in-law is going back to her people and her gods. Go back with her."

But Ruth replied, "Don't urge me to leave you or to turn back from you. Where you go I will go, and where you stay I will stay. Your people will be my people and your God my God. Where you die, I will die, and there I will be buried. May the Lord deal with me, be it ever so severely, if anything but death separates you and me." When Naomi realized that Ruth was determined to go with her, she stopped urging her.

One of the main themes of this series is that the issue of power must be dealt with in relationships rather than misguided notions of love and romance that camouflage the actual distribution of power. Real love is about the fair and equitable distribution of power in a relationship. But often we cannot ascertain real love because we are blinded by popular notions of love and romance. One of the most powerful tools that enables us to be blinded by popular notions of love and romance is excessive melodrama.

Melodrama is the extreme glorification and need of a relationship in one's life beyond the bounds of what is rational, right, or true. Melodrama is the overexaggerated need for relationship such that one makes relationship and the issues that surround it matters of life and death. Melodrama is typically about women's trials and sorrows in love and relationship. Melodrama is about the fusion of romance, love, sex, and reproduction in an attempt to discover meaning. Melodrama at its root exalts and portrays female innocence in a very structured way: all girls and women as innocent, all men as dogs, and relationships as matters of life and death. One can see melodrama on television every day, and excessive melodrama, at that—tales about innocent women dogged by men; tales about girls cutting their wrists because of a boyfriend; tales about a woman getting revenge because another woman "stole her man." Melodrama depicts and exalts relationships as matters of life and death.

The Book of Ruth portrays women who are not excessively melodramatic, so they are not making the center of their lives a love relationship with a man. While it is true that Naomi and Ruth are widows, their story, at least at the point of our text, is about their relationship with one another. Their story allows us to focus on women as people, women with a sense of self, women without the number one issue in their lives being whether or not they have a man, are trying to get a man, need a man, have been left by a man, were hurt by a man, or want a man. These women have learned to think about themselves.

In a way, the story of Ruth is not really about Ruth. It was probably written to tell how Ruth helped establish the lineage of David, from which Christ was descended. However, the story does provide an instructive glimpse of how Ruth and Naomi felt about their predicament and thought about themselves, and it shows us how they dealt with their lives. Therefore, we can learn a great deal about men and women and the development of self and personal power from this text, and we can learn about the temptation to be excessively melodramatic.

In the days of the judges, around 800 B.C., there was a famine in the land. A man named Elimelech and his wife, Naomi, left Bethlehem in Judea and went to Moab with their two sons to try to get some food and make a living. When the family had lived for a while in Moab, Elimelech died, leaving Naomi and their sons. The two sons married women named Ruth and Orpah, but after about ten years, the sons died, leaving Ruth and Orpah widowed, like Naomi.

Following the death of her husband and sons, Naomi heard that the Lord had come to the rescue of Bethlehem and Judah, so she decided to go back home. She packed her belongings and started on her way, taking Ruth and Orpah with her. As daughters-in-law, Ruth and Orpah showed kindness in their willingness to accompany Naomi at least part of the way. They could have tried to persuade her to continue to live in Moab, but she had resolved to go home, so they seemingly were resolved to respect her decision and even to go with her as far as the border of Moab.

See them as they are leaving town. See them coming out of the land of Moab. Suddenly Naomi looked at her two daughters-in-law and said, "Let me bless you. You have done what daughters-in-law ought to do. You have stayed with me, and you have kept me. You have respected the memory of your husbands. You have done well, but I think you should go back to your people. I think you should go back home."

Then she blessed them. "May the LORD show kindness to you, as you have shown to your dead and to me" (Ruth 1:8, NIV). Next she kissed them, and the Bible says they wept aloud when she kissed them. They wept aloud. So touching was the kiss; so touching was the love; so touching was the compassion. So touching was their relationship that the pain of separation forced them to weep aloud. The Bible says that the women said, "We'll go all the way back to Bethlehem of Judea with you." And Naomi, because she loved her daughters-in-law, said, "No. Don't go home with me. Why would you go home with me? What will you do? I am not going to marry another husband. Are you going to wait for me to get another husband so I can have some more sons? Are you going to wait for those sons to grow up so you can remarry? No. Go on and live your life. Go on and do your own thing. Go on to where God takes you. Go on. Go on. Go on."

At this they wept again, the text says (Ruth 1:14). They wept out loud. These women had been with and supported each other in the mutual grief over the loss of their husbands. Now they were grieving the loss of each other. The Bible says that Orpah kissed her mother-in-law and left. But Ruth clung, saying, "Wherever you go, I will go; And wherever you lodge, I will lodge; Your people shall be my people, and your God, my God" (Ruth 1:16, NKJV).

We are most familiar with Ruth. Traditionally Orpah is dismissed as the one who made the wrong choice while Ruth is honored for her decision to leave everything, including her people, and cleave to Naomi. Ruth responds the way many of us would to love: by giving up everything and cleaving to another. Ruth is also exalted by some people because of her choice, which resulted in her being saved. According to this perspective, Ruth became part of David's lineage, from whence the Messiah came, while Orpah chose to return to her foreign gods. Ruth took the more spiritual path while Orpah took the path of idolatry and paganism. But let's take a look at Orpah to see what her choice can teach us about how to love and preserve ourselves, how to love and go in our own direction. Orpah did not love Naomi any less than did Ruth. Orpah simply made a different choice than Ruth did. She decided to go home. It is possible to love as deeply as the one who cleaves but still choose to go home.

A look at Orpah helps us to explore the idea that *a self is more attractive than no self.* Issues or concerns will present themselves in almost every relationship, and when this happens one has an opportunity to declare a position, to take a stand, and to declare one's self. When significant issues come up in a relationship and one will not declare one's self but will duck instead, the relationship will take over him or her. The more one ducks, the more the relationship will take over the person until he or she will get to the point of being entirely taken over, losing all sense of self.

If someone will not declare herself and her position, declare what she believes, what she thinks, and how she feels but will continue instead to compromise principle just to get along, then she will begin to lose who she is. She will begin to doubt whether she is intelligent. She will begin to doubt whether she can think. She will begin to doubt whether she can live without a man. She will be stuck on stupid.

Women are not the only ones who are stuck on stupid. Men also are stuck on stupid. Men may point to women in their lives who have no self, but I have discovered that if a man is married to a woman who does not have a self, his sense of self is suspect too, for people with about the same level of self tend to marry each other. That is one of the reasons folks are attracted to one another. They have about the same level of maturity, so a lot of men are deep into no self.

Workaholism is a form of no self. Alcoholism is a form of no self. Affairism is a form of no self. Having no self means that a person has compromised and ducked significant concerns in the relationship for so long that he or she has been swallowed up. Once people are swallowed up, they are stuck on stupid.

Put two people in a room, and close the door. There is only so much oxygen in that room. If one person uses more than his share of the oxygen, then the other person will not have enough for her circulatory system and brain. If the circulatory system does not have enough oxygen to feed vital organs, the body will go stupid. The person who will not claim his or her position (or share of oxygen) is in emotional terms stuck on stupid. The person who does not take in enough oxygen is intelligent but emotionally stupid. Got a big bank account, but stupid. Big executive on the job, but stupid. Big pastor with a big church, but stupid. Got robes on, but stuck on stupid.

Stuck on stupid is an emotional position, resulting in one not knowing what one is doing or where one is going. You see, a sense of self is that which preserves one's organism. And when people lose their selves, they lose the operating system that coordinates everything they have. So it does not matter how a person looks if she is stuck on stupid. It does not matter how big a bank account he has if he is stuck on stupid. It does not matter where our parents came from if we are stuck on stupid. It does not matter what neighborhood we live in or who our pastor is if we are stuck on stupid.

When we lose ourselves, we become unattractive. Here she is giving up herself to get a man, and that's unattractive to the man she is getting. Some change is necessary and desirable in a negotiated relationship, especially for a Christian, but losing one's self just to keep the peace, changing one's self to pacify, losing one's self, being a doormat . . . that's unattractive! Going along with everything is unattractive. Losing one's self to a job is unattractive. Alcoholism is unattractive. To lose one's self is unattractive because when we lose ourselves, we lose at least seven vital characteristics of living, identity of purpose, and meaning.

We Lose Our Resourcefulness

First, we become unattractive because we lose our resourcefulness. Resourcefulness is the repertoire of creative responses that a person brings to any given situation. It is the ability to come up with a way to get something done despite barriers and roadblocks. For example, if a person lacks money to go to school but is resourceful, he will exploit his wide repertoire of responses to the situation rather than settling for a negative, can't-do response. As a resourceful person, he will discover that he can respond with faith. He will discover that he can respond by seeking scholarship information. He will discover that he can respond by thinking about work-study options or many other hopeful responses, but when a person loses himself to someone else's agenda and interpretation of reality and when he continues to duck from his own sense of integrity, then he loses his attractiveness. It is not just the body that makes one attractive. It is not just how much one earns that makes one attractive. You see, it is the quality of resourcefulness that helps make one attractive.

We Lose Our Humor

Second, we lose our humor. A key component in the life of unhappy people is that humorless type of seriousness. When people keep ducking, they lose their humor. They are no fun to be with because they are serious all the time. They need to lighten up. Life is not always that serious. Humor, lightheartedness, and laughter are strong ingredients of attractiveness. If we continue to say nothing when something really matters to us and we keep telling only half the truth when we have a whole lot of other feelings and thoughts to share, we will lose our humor.

We Lose Our Savvy

Third, we lose our savvy. Savvy is the ability to quickly adjust one's emotional map to handle the realities of life. For instance, when I came out of seminary, I was very naïve. I began to teach a preaching class in seminary. After the first session I came back home, and my wife asked, "How did the class go?" I said, "They're green, like lambs being led to the slaughter. They don't have a clue." And my wife said, "That's just how you were." That was so true. When I came out of seminary I thought that everybody wanted to grow spiritually. I thought that everybody wanted to become a tither. I thought that everybody wanted to go to Bible class. I thought that everybody in the church was attuned to the cause of Christ. I thought that everyone wanted to move forward. Now I think that some of us want to move forward. Some of us want to grow in Christ. Some of us want to grow spiritually. I developed some savvy.

I could have been crushed when the reality of church life hit me, and in some places I was and still am, but I have enough savvy to make it, to adjust my map to the reality of the direction the world is traveling in. This relates to the whole question of innocence, and how some women, particularly, who come out of sheltered homes get blindsided by unsheltered men. Women need to have some savvy and learn fast.

We Lose Our Persistence

Fourth, we lose our persistence, which is the ability to chart our course according to our measurements rather than relying on the use of someone else's map. Many of us must rely on others to tell us exactly where we are in relationship to our goals. Therefore, we depend on others' directions to let us know when to speed up, slow down, or change course. But some people have the uncanny ability to know where they are according to their own reckoning. They are able to persist because they continually update their course based upon their inner compass rather than take a look over someone else's shoulder or a peek at someone else's map.

We Lose Our Ingenuity

Fifth, we lose our ingenuity, the ability to ask new questions. It is not just the ability to come up with new answers to old questions that is important, but the ability to reframe old questions into new ones. I have come to understand that questions are more important than answers because answers change but questions remain eternal. The range of answers that is possible is predetermined by the kinds of questions that are asked. Ingenuity is the ability to ask new questions.

We Lose Our Inner World

Sixth, we lose the capacity to preserve our inner world. The virus has come in so deep to the host that the virus is at the heart of the host, replicating itself. The originator of Negro History Week (now Black History Month), Carter G. Woodson, said it this way: "Many Negroes have such an inferiority complex that when they no longer have to go to the back door, they go back there and cut one for themselves" (paraphrase). Because the virus is down at the center of the host, replicating itself, we don't have the ability to preserve our inner world. When the virus gets down into our thinking, down into our spirit, down into our soul, negativity takes over. The host then begins to act out the negativity even if no one is around to make the host behave in a self-destructive manner.

Preserve your inner world. The inner world is a place where you can get in contact with God. How much solitary confinement can you stand? Consider former South African President Nelson Mandela, who remained in prison for twenty-seven years and came out stronger than when he went in because he had something on the inside that allowed him to preserve his inner world. Consider author Viktor Frankl, who stated that while he was in a Nazi concentration camp, he visualized himself giving lectures about his experience there. The guards could whip his body, but they could not control his inner world.

How much solitary confinement can you stand? The host is so infected by the virus that the host's inner world gets entered by the virus, and it begins to replicate itself. Then, not only do we not have a self; we invent ways to be more no self.

We Lose Our Imaginative Capacity

Seventh, we lose our imaginative capacity. The problem is not that we have problems. The problem is that we do not have the imagination to see beyond our problems. That is the problem. The more stressed out one becomes about problems, the less imagination one has to overcome them. When we are stuck in our imaginative capacity, we need to come to church to get hooked up with God because God sees all of the possibilities for a situation and may drop one in our spirits or communicate very clearly to us, "Hang around with me, and sooner or later I will break forth in your spirit." New possibility.

Now, let us locate Orpah. She went home, I believe, because to go with Naomi would have been to stifle her resourcefulness, to stifle her humor, to stifle her savvy, to stifle her ingenuity, to stifle her persistence, to stifle her capacity to preserve her own inner world, and to stifle her capacity to be imaginative. That is why she went home. It wasn't that she did not love Naomi. She did love Naomi, but her love for Naomi did not mean that she should lose her self. You see, it is not about whether you go or stay. It is about whether or not what you are doing is preserving a sense of self.

We are into looks, so the couple has been together fifty years and they look like they are happy, while the divorcee is a sinner because she left him after five years. Well, I don't know about that. I don't want to be blasphemous, *but it is possible to stay and look happy but be stuck on stupid. And it is possible to leave and discover self.* People often ask their pastors, "Well, what do you think we ought to do?" We pastors don't know. We are trying to figure out what we are going to do in our lives. We don't know. You had better get God. You had better find the one who has imaginative capacity.

Sometimes couples come in and say, "Do you think I should stay, or do you think I should go?" Well, how are you going to decide that? They try making a little list. What's good? What's bad? They list all the good things and then all the bad things. If the good things outweigh the bad things, they stay; if the bad things outweigh the good things, they go. The problem with this approach is that the good and the bad change from week to week, so it is not about making a list. It is about asking questions about the distribution of power in the relationship: Does the relationship give me room to develop my resourcefulness? To develop my humor? To develop my savvy? To develop my ingenuity? To develop my persistence? To preserve my inner world? To develop my imaginative capacity? That is how you decide. You ask questions about the power in the relationship and whether the relationship grants the power to develop one's self.

I wonder, in our excessive melodrama, if we do not make too much out of love and romance. I wonder if it is not really about love but about being attractive. A self is more attractive. Orpah was a more attractive person going home. Ruth was a more attractive person staying with Naomi, and so neither choice is wrong. It is not whether you ought to be single or you ought to be with somebody. It is a question of what makes you more attractive. For some of us, it is more healthy to be by ourselves and develop ourselves. For others, it is more healthy to be in relationship developing ourselves. Stop judging on externals, whether somebody has a man or does not have a man. Having a man is six in one hand and six in the other. Being single is six in one hand and six in the other. Being called to a small church is six in one hand and six in the other. Being at a big church is six in one hand and six in the other. No one thing is right for everybody. It is not about what condition we find ourselves in but whether we, as individuals, use that experience or condition to develop more attractive selves.

When you are stuck on stupid, the best thing to do is to cry unto God, and the God of all mercy, the God of all compassion, will hear your cry. God will ask you, "What about your resourcefulness? I gave you that. Where has it gone? What about your humor? I gave you that. Where has it gone? What about your savvy? I made you with that. Where has it gone? What about your ingenuity? You were made with that. Where has it gone? What about your persistence? I'm not going to solve any problems for you when I have given you all of these resources and you are just sitting on them. What about your capacity to preserve your own inner world? What about your own imaginative capacity?"

Some prosperity preachers will promise you that God is on the side of wealth and blessing. I am suggesting that God is on the side of resourcefulness, humor, savvy, ingenuity, the preservation of your inner world, and your imaginative capacity. Sometimes God will supernaturally enter your situation and the persons whom you are grappling with will change in miraculous ways, fulfilling your hopes. But most of the time, God expects you and me to use the power that has already been given to us. God works for us to develop our power and attractiveness. God was at work in Orpah's life then, developing her power and attractiveness, and God is at work in our lives now, developing our power and attractiveness.

Study Questions

1. Orpah, in the Book of Ruth, decides that it is better for her to return to her own people than to go back to Israel with her mother-in-law, Naomi. In doing so, Dr. Thomas says, Orpah demonstrates the attractiveness of having a self, or being free to declare one's position. Discuss Orpah's decision. Compare it with Ruth's.

2. Why do women, particularly, tend to find more virtue in Ruth's decision than in Orpah's?

3. Case study: A young college student received a full scholarship to attend a university in another state. On the day that she was to leave home, her mother took her to the airport, but just as the young woman was about to board the airplane, her mother began to cry hysterically, saying that she did not know what she would do if her daughter were to leave the family. The young woman turned back and went back home to stay. At the last moment, she enrolled in a local junior college. She said that she had not previously realized how important she was to her family. Discuss the young woman's action. Was it her decision or a reaction? What might be some future repercussions or benefits of this action?

4. Stuck on stupid, says Dr. Thomas, is an emotional position of being swallowed up by another person that causes one to lose attractiveness. Dr. Thomas says that attractiveness is composed of the following qualities: resourcefulness, humor, savvy, persistence, ingenuity, inner world, and imaginative capacity. Rate your attractiveness in one or more relationships, based on these qualities.

5. While we celebrate wedding anniversaries, longevity is not necessarily a sign of a healthy marriage relationship. The author says that some

marriages survive only because one of the partners has given up claims to himself or herself. Would it be more appropriate to celebrate something other than, or in addition to, the years a couple has been together? If so, what things or qualities of relationship might we celebrate?

6. How can we affirm God's gift to us of the seven qualities of personal attractiveness?

Prayer Thought: I will endeavor in every one of my relationships to be true to myself.

Chapter Four

Waiting
to
Exhale

Genesis 2:4-7, NIV

This is the account of the heavens and the earth when they were created.

When the LORD GOD made the earth and the heavens—and no shrub of the field had yet appeared on the earth and no plant of the field had yet sprung up, for the LORD GOD had not sent rain on the earth and there was no man to work the ground, but streams came up from the earth and watered the whole surface of the ground—the LORD GOD formed the man from the dust of the ground and breathed into his nostrils the breath of life, and the man became a living being.

And the Lord God formed man from the dust of the ground and breathed into his nostrils the breath of life, and we became living beings, waiting to exhale. This text teaches us that after the Lord God made the heavens and the earth, the earth was dry and parched like a desert. There was no shrub of the field or plant of the ground because the Lord God had not yet sent rain upon the earth. There also was no one to work the ground, so the earth was dry and parched like a desert.

The text says that the Lord God allowed mists to come up from the ground and water the whole surface of the earth. God did not cause rain to fall, but God pressed the button on the divine sprinkler system and nozzles popped out of the ground to water the whole earth. This means that the dry desert was watered, and it became slimy like mud. The Bible says that God took the mud and formed humanity from the wet dust of the ground. We were the unformed clay, spinning on a potter's wheel that God molded and shaped, defined and refined, until we were fashioned into an awesome work of art. But when God stepped back from the work of art, something was still missing. We were a house but not yet a home. We were dressed up, but we didn't have anywhere to go. We were a shell, but we did not have life. The text says that God breathed the breath of life into us, and we became living souls. God exhaled, and we became living beings. We could breathe and have life only because God breathed.

This text teaches us that there were two stages to creation: the forming and finishing of the clay and the breathing of the breath of life. It often seems that so much of this world wants to return humanity to the wet dust of the first stage of creation where we are just a shell but not a life; a figurine but not a soul; a mannequin but not a person of significance; formed and finished clay but not a breath. And because we so often buy the paradigms of this world, we perceive ourselves to have no breath, or we perceive ourselves to have no consent to breathe. The effect of this is that many of us hold our breath. Many of us learn when not to breathe at all—just to hold our breath. We learn how to go back to the first stage of creation. We learn how to live and not have life. We learn how to live and not breathe. We learn how to live and not have hopes. We learn how to live and not have dreams. We learn how to return to the first stage of creation. We give ourselves and don't get much back, so we learn to hold our breath.

We try to talk, but it seems nobody can hear us, so we learn how to hold our breath. We work our fingers to the bone but do not feel appreciated for our work, so we hold our breath. We take care of so many people but receive so little care ourselves, so we hold our breath. We have learned how to return to the first stage of creation. We have learned how to not breathe.

Some of us have relationships with people who use up more than their share of oxygen, and rather than demand our share of oxygen, we simply do not breathe. We are waiting to exhale. We know that we are dead, so we try to exhale, but we're exhaling in all the wrong places. Women try to exhale with men. Men try to exhale with women. We try to exhale with large houses and big jobs. We try to exhale with designer clothes, gym shoes, and labels. We try to exhale with drugs. We try to exhale with alcohol. We know we are asphyxiated. We know we don't have enough air. We just want to breathe. We just want to have a life with hopes and dreams.

What we need to do is exhale by ourselves and for ourselves. We cannot breathe for other people; we can exhale only for ourselves. If we learn how to exhale, we will be surprised to see how many people there are for us to exhale with.

I am talking about demanding one's share of oxygen in the room. I am not talking about taking more than one's share, but I am also not talking about taking less than one's share. I am asking, "Why are we waiting to exhale? Why are we waiting to breathe?" The text says that *God* breathed on us, and we became a living being. When God breathed on us, we had life, and when we had life, we had to inhale and exhale as a part of the rhythm of living. So I want to know why we are waiting to exhale. Why do we store up all of the exhaling we want to do and put false hopes in other people when God, who created us to become living souls, has given us the right and the ability to exhale?

I believe that we all have the right to say what we think, feel, and believe. I believe that persons cannot exist if they cannot say what they think, feel, and believe. That is what it means to exhale. To exhale is to claim one's own space, to have one's own thoughts, to feel one's own feelings, to believe one's own beliefs, to speak one's own peace. That is what it is to breathe: to have the right to speak one's mind without being judged, or put down, or beat upon, or slapped, or made to feel stupid because of one's opinions. God has given us these rights, and nobody can take them away from us or intimidate us.

I have the right to say what I think, feel, and believe, and somebody else has the right to disagree; yet I have the right to not change my opinion because of someone else's disagreement, or if I so choose, to change it. I have the right.

One of the good members of the church whom I cared about, nurtured, and loved deeply decided to leave the church. Typically, when somebody tells me that he or she is leaving the church, I become defensive and ask "What's wrong?" because I assume that something is wrong with me or the church. But this time I did not ask that question. Instead I asked the person what was going on, and the reply was, "I'm no longer growing spiritually here." Previously I would have tried to convert and convince the member; I would have tried to show the person how spiritual growth could take place in the church, but something in me said, "Say this," so I said to the person, "I understand, and if I were not growing here, I would leave, too." In other words, this is your life. I don't have a right to override what you think, what you feel, and what you believe. If I stop growing as the pastor of the church, I may leave, too, because my priority in life is to grow spiritually and to mature. I want to grow up in Christ. I don't want to be the same person I used to be, so if I am not growing spiritually, I need to consider leaving, too.

It is possible to be yourself and to breathe. It is possible to claim your own space and not be guilty of invading other people's space. You see, we are confused. When somebody says, "Have a self," we hear the word *selfish*, which connotes that one is so concerned with one's own agenda that he or she will run over everybody else to get it done. I am not talking about being selfish. I am talking about having a self. I am talking about having thoughts, feelings, and beliefs that are one's own. You, the individual, thought them through, and it is not your interest to convert, to persuade, or to coerce other people to think like you think. I am not talking about being selfish. I am not talking about being self-indulgent. I am talking about being possessed of self. I am not talking about being self-centered, so that the whole universe revolves around one's self. I am talking about being self-confident, having some confidence in what one thinks, what one believes, what one wants to do with his or her life, where one wants to go, and what God intended for one.

I am not talking about being self-conscious all the time, so that one can't do anything for trying so hard to please everybody. I am talking about being self-aware so that when people give one feedback about one's self, one can be aware of the feedback, take it in, think about it, pray about it, process it, and decide what to do.

I am not talking about being self-serving. I am talking about self-respect. I am talking about a self. I am talking about one's right to breathe. I'm talking about one's right to claim one's own space, one's right to fit, to feel, to believe, to express an individual opinion. I am talking about one's right to be self-evident and not hidden. I am talking about the right one has to make one's self, to explain one's self, to be one's self, to love one's self, to take care of one's self. The right to be a person. The right to breathe.

Sly Stone sang, "I thank you for letting me be myself." But if someone doesn't let me be myself, I will still be myself because being myself is like breathing, and if I am not myself, I will die. If I don't know myself, if I don't have myself, if I don't own myself, if I don't possess myself, if I don't live myself, I don't have anything. All I have is a person who is being asphyxiated, who is dying, who is scuffling and struggling. I am talking about having a self. I am not saying that one should not love, that one ought not to be self-sacrificing, but what I am talking about is love on top of a self. With a self, I can look after my life. I can look after my soul. I can look after my happiness. I can look after my joy.

We might do well to spend less time trying to convert people than to be clear about what we think and feel. Once people hear what we think, they have the right to agree or disagree. You see, one of the reasons why many of us don't like the word *decision* is because it comes from the Latin *decaedere*, meaning "to cut." When one decides something, one cuts something. *De-ci-sion*. A lot of us are not decisive because we don't like to cut, and because we don't like to cut, we're trying to keep everybody and everything. When a person makes a decision, other people have to decide what they're going to do based on that decision. They might be unhappy with the decision, but that's all right. That's just the opportunity for them to be clear about what they think, feel, and believe. Such clarity is often the opportunity for the other person to exercise a sense of self.

Consider this. When people say, "This is what I think, and feel, and believe," know that they are not truly exhaling if they have to impose their thoughts, feelings, and beliefs on someone else. For example, my wife and I drove all night to visit my grandmother in Mississippi. When we arrived, I jumped out of the car, excited to see my grandmother, and hugged her. The first thing she said to me was "Ministers don't wear shorts." That was the *first* thing she said after we had driven for sixteen hours to see her. So I said to her, "*This* minister wears shorts."

When people are telling you about you, they are not telling you about themselves. It would have been entirely appropriate for my grandmother to say, "*I* believe that ministers ought not to wear shorts," and I could have said, "Well, *you* have the right to believe that; *I* just disagree with what *you* believe, and *I* have to do what *I* think is right." Then we could have gone on and had black-eyed peas and grouper fish. But my grandmother and I got into it, right off the bat. The right to be me. To have my own thoughts. To have my own feelings. People have a right to be clear with us about what they think, and we have the right to agree or disagree. That's what I am talking about—breathing. That's what I am talking about—exhaling. I am talking about being clear about what we think, what we believe, what we're willing to stand on. That's exhaling. That's what I'm talking about.

Why do we have this right? We have this right because God gave it to us. The text says that God breathed the breath of life, and the man became a living being. God breathed, and I became me. I became myself. God gave me a self. God gave me a right. I don't have to give it up to be in a relationship with anybody. I learned this lesson the hard way.

I sat watching at the foot of my wife's bed in the delivery room, and when that child came out of her womb, the doctor grabbed the baby, called the code blue team, and went to another room where they started to work on our daughter. However, she died. After she died, I learned that she was able to live as long as she was breathing the liquid of the womb, but when she came out of the womb and had to breathe air, she could not live because she had what was called a diaphragmatic hernia, a hole in the diaphragm that caused her heart and her lungs to grow together. Therefore, she couldn't breathe, so the doctor had to perform surgery on her lungs, but the surgery was unsuccessful, and she died on the operating table.

This is what I learned. The mother can bring a baby as far as she can in the womb. The mother can eat the right foods, and drink the right drinks, and can get the right kind of rest. She can have that little bit of control, but after she has done all of that and the baby leaves the womb, God has to give the baby life. When the baby has to make a transition from the liquid in the womb to the breath of air, God has to breathe on that child so that he or she becomes a *living* soul.

When we make the transition from the liquid in the womb to the breath of the air, we receive ourselves and the right to exhale.

We are waiting to exhale because we are looking for air on the outside. We are looking for validation from the outside. We are waiting for people to tell us that we look good. We are waiting for folks to be impressed with our cars and our houses. From the outside with our outfits. From the outside with our country clubs. From the outside with our middle class-ness. From the outside with our friends. From the outside impressing others.

We're looking for rain to fall. The text says, "The LORD God had not sent rain on the earth." We're looking for compliments to rain down. We're looking for affirmation to rain down. We're looking for friendliness to rain down, kindness and love. We want it to rain down, and that's all right, but the text says that the mists came up *out* of the earth. The water came up from the midst of the earth and watered the ground.

Stop looking for somebody to rain on you. Stop looking for

someone to water your garden. The water must come from the inside. And the one who sends his or her shaft down deep enough will find springs of living water, welling up into everlasting life!

Dr. Howard Thurman tells about his traveling to a desert. He said he looked around and almost everything was dead, but every now and then he would come across green trees in the desert. And he said he wondered about that: How could green trees grow in a parched, in a dry, in a desert land? He said he found the answer to his question when he read about the desert in a magazine article. The article said that way down beneath the desert were streams of living water, and some trees send their roots down deep enough to be able to tap into that water.

He who sends his shaft down deep enough in God will find streams of living water, and the water will come up and water that life from the inside. Oh, there will be desert on the outside, but that life will be watered from the inside. That one will be exhaling from the inside. That one will be breathing from the inside.

Someone may lose his job, but he'll have deep roots and streams of living water on the inside. Someone may lose a relationship or some friends, but she'll have streams of living water on the inside. That's what I'm talking about. Send your shaft down deep enough. Get down deep in God. Stop practicing surface and superficial religion. Stop looking to human beings, trying to exhale with some man, trying to exhale with some woman, trying to exhale with your gym shoes, trying to exhale with your reputation. The one who sends his shaft down deep enough won't have to wait to exhale.

Prayer: God, help us today to not be coercive of others but to work in our own heads to clear our own thinking, to clear our own position, to clear our own beliefs, to clear our own hopes. I thank you for the process. Some of us are working to get free. We aren't free yet, but we're trying to get there. Some of us read the sermon, and we're trying some of what we read. We may have fallen flat on our faces, but we're ready to try again. We're trying again. We thank you for the privilege.

When we send our shafts down deep enough, plant our roots down deep enough, we will run into you, who gave us the breath of life. When we send our shafts down deep enough, we will run into you, who said, "You used to be a clay pot, but I breathed into you the breath of life, and you became a living soul." We would send our shafts down deep enough in you. Send them down, send them down, and let us exhale.

In the blessed name of Jesus. Amen.

Study Questions

1. To exhale is to claim one's own space, to feel one's own feelings, to have one's own thoughts, to believe one's own beliefs, and to speak one's own peace, says Dr. Thomas. This principle is at the heart of democracy. What are some issues in the church and society today that argue for the ability to exhale? (Examples: the ordaining into ministry and the marrying of homosexual people; women as senior pastors)

2. What is the difference between exhaling to find one's self and being selfish or self-centered?

3. How does the claiming of one's own space improve the family, the group, the community?

4. Reread the story in this chapter about Dr. Thomas's grandmother, who objected to his wearing shorts because he was a minister. Read 1 Corinthians 10:23-33. Is it ever appropriate to lay aside one's prerogative to be oneself for the good of others? If so, in what kinds of situations would one say with Paul, "All things are lawful, but not all things are expedient"?

5. What can Christians and others of good will in democratic societies do to help people in other countries who are struggling to obtain freedom of expression?

Prayer Thought: Exhaling is the freedom that I have to decide when and when not to exercise my prerogatives.

Chapter Five

A Time
for
Letting Go

Ecclesiastes 3:1-8, NIV

There is a time for everything, and a season for every activity under heaven:

a time to be born and a time to die,

a time to plant and a time to uproot, . . .

a time to tear down and a time to build, . . .

a time to mourn and a time to dance, . . .

a time to embrace and a time to refrain,

a time to search and a time to give up,

a time to keep and a time to throw away, . . .

And for my purposes, a time to love and a time to let go.
The writer of Ecclesiastes is attempting to teach a critical life lesson in this text. The writer understood that there is an appropriate time for every action and reaction under the sun. The writer reminds us that life has many seasons, and though we prefer the seemingly positive seasons of planting, building, laughing, and birthing, seasons of uprooting, dying, tearing down, and refraining are positive as well. It is difficult for us to accept dying, tearing down, and uprooting as positive life experiences. I want to explore the time for letting go as positive. I believe one of the most critical decisions in our lives is when to love by letting go. In accordance with the writer of Ecclesiastes, Tina Turner

teaches us much about a time for letting go.

From the deep recesses of my mind, I hear Tina Turner's profound and penetrating question, "What's love got to do with it?" It is a question that gets at the core of living for each and every one of us: What does love have to do with life? What is the purpose, meaning, and value of love to our lives? Tina is on *Oprah*, and I am glued for the whole hour watching Tina, listening to Tina, feeling Tina, and experiencing Tina. Tina Turner is so deep and expansive in our culture that she is all around me. I am in a strange city, alone, preaching revival, homesick, and scanning the radio for familiar music. All of a sudden, Tina on the radio, singing words that I cannot forget, "I don't care who's wrong or right. I don't really want to fight no more. There's a time for letting go."[1] What does love have to do with a time for letting go?

I rent the video and watch Tina Turner in *What's Love Got to Do with It?* I watch Tina struggle with the time for letting go. In the movie, her husband, Ike Turner, is abusive toward her, and she struggles to let go of him and what she previously understood as love. It is clear, however, that Tina has a weakness for Ike that is connected to her own childhood abandonment issues; hence, her wounded understanding of love. Because she had not worked through the pain of being abandoned in her life, she found it extremely difficult to let go of what she thought was love, even when love was abusive. She could not reconcile violence and hate masquerading as love, but neither could she walk away. She was discovering that there is a time for letting go.

Tina Turner singing now in my CD player and headphones—a time for letting go. She says again: "I don't care who's wrong or right. I don't really want to fight no more. There's a time for letting go." I understand better now what she means after watching the movie. I interpret her to say through the song: In this abusive relationship masquerading as love, I don't care about blame. I don't care what you did or what I didn't do. I don't even care who is wrong or right. There is a time and place for love but also a time and a place for letting go. I have decided to let go. On Oprah's show Tina said it best, "This song perfectly summarizes a large part of my life: a time for letting go." It summarizes a large part of my life, too. There is a time to love and a time to love through letting go.

I am not sure that we know a whole lot about letting go. Someone once said that in matters of love we only need to practice letting go, for holding on comes easily, and we do not need to learn it. We already know in matters of love how to clutch, how to grab tight, and how to hold on. We need in love to learn how to let people go. We need to learn how to let go of that part of a relationship that is violence and hate masquerading as love. We must let go of the part of ourselves that holds on to violence and hate as love and allows another to get away with things that are harmful to us. There is a time for working on our vulnerability to someone. There is a time for working on our weakness for someone. There is a time for turning someone off in us. There is a time to protect ourselves and love ourselves. There is a time for letting go.

It is hard for many of us to deal with, but we are weak for certain people. It is hard to face, but the truth is that when we are taken advantage of, it has something to do with our weakness for the person and the fact that we went beyond the point of letting go. A mother is weak for a son, and she keeps bailing him out, and each time she bails him out, she uses more of her savings. She doesn't have much, but she continues to bail him out. Now she's almost down to nothing, so he calls one last time, and she gives him all that she has ever worked for and earned in this world. He squanders it, and she is left penniless and broke. Some would say that he ruined her, but what about the fact that she was weak for him? What about the fact that she did not protect and love herself? What about the fact that she went beyond the time for letting go? What does love have to do with it? What does love have to do with a time for letting go?

It is helpful to compare our understanding of love with the immune system in our body. Negative people and relationships that masquerade hate and violence as love can be labeled as viruses. We spend a whole lot of time blaming the virus. We want to get mad at viruses, but viruses are just viruses. Viruses have an inability to regulate themselves, and they wreak havoc according to their nature. More important than the virus is the immune system that has the responsibility to regulate, control, and limit the harm of viruses. What about the immunological response of the host to the virus? If a virus takes us over, what about the response of our immune system? Our tendency is to focus on the virus, call it love, and not focus on the response of the immune system.

Your understanding of love has a tremendous impact on your immune system. If you accept hate and violence as love, it compromises your immune system. As your immune system is compromised, the virus replicates and begins to produce itself in you. The virus will weaken you so much that you will give up everything, you will lose everything, and you will in your confusion justify the absolute losing of your life, purpose, and direction (your self) as love. What does love have to do with it? What does love have to do with violence and abuse? What does love have to do with a time for letting go? There is a time for letting go.

When Tina Turner says, "I don't care who is wrong or right. I don't want to fight anymore, there is a time for letting go," I understand Tina to mean, I am going to work on my own immune system. I am going to work on my own self. I am going to work on my own responses. There is a time for letting go of trying to change you; trying to make you into something that I want you to be; trying to get you to do this or that; trying to get you to straighten up; trying to get you to quit doing this; trying to get you to stop drugging; trying to get you to stop drinking; trying to get you to stop hitting me; trying to get you to go to work; trying to get you to love me. . . . There is a time for letting go. There is a time for working on our vulnerability to someone. There is a time for working on our weakness for someone. There is a time for realizing that what you call love is destructive to me, and I never have to accept what is destructive to me. There is a time for letting go.

Maybe this is the greatest kind of courage: to face the fact that when we are taken advantage of, it is because we compromised our immune system and went past the point of letting go. We are so angry with our ex for treating us a certain way, and while it might be all right to be angry, at least one factor in the discussion ought to be that the ex got away with so much because of our inadequate immune response. We did not understand that a part of love was letting go. There is a time for letting go.

Now that we agree that a part of love is letting go, let's talk about the process of letting go. There is a time for letting go, but that time is a process. It takes many of us a considerable amount of time to let go. It takes time and a process to let go of the sickness in me that attracts and tolerates viruses and infected people in my life as agents of harm. Many of us do not let go overnight; it takes extended time and a thorough process. I believe that there are five stages in the process of letting go.

Letting Go Hurts

The first stage is the admission that letting go is going to hurt. When the reality of the destructive nature of love hits us and we begin to think about letting go, we also become aware that letting go is going to hurt. There is no way that one is going to get out of a chronic situation without an acute phase of pain. We realize that it is going to hurt to stay, and it will hurt to let go. There is no painless option. The only question is which option is healthy pain. When a medical doctor treats a chronic condition, the medical doctor will take the patient through an acute phase called surgery. Surgery is painful, but the acute phase is induced for the removal of the chronic condition. Letting go is accepting an acute phase of hurt.

Letting Go Means Risking the Loss of Important Things

The second stage of letting go is to accept the reality that you must risk the loss of things that are important to you. Letting go will involve sacrifice. We will have to lose something that is important to us. Some people stay in bad relationships because they do not believe that they can make it on their own. Some people stay because without the relationship they will not have the same standard of living. Some people stay because they might lose face. They've had one divorce, and this will be the second one, and they don't want to feel like they are relationship failures. Some people stay because they don't want to lose the illusion of romance. Even though the relationship is toxic and it is killing them, they cannot leave because they will have to give up something important to them. If they cannot give up what is important to them, they are held hostage by their belief. In order to let go, we are going to have to give up a vision, a dream, a belief, a way of thinking that is dear to us.

Letting Go Means Doing Surgery on One's Self

The third stage of letting go is the discovery that one must do surgery on one's self. In the first two stages, I realize how painful letting go is. In the third stage, I make the conscious choice to confront myself and go through the pain. I do not challenge the virus, but I challenge myself and induce the acute phase. I decide to risk losing many things that are important to me. I make the choice. It is the choice to confront one's self, to be honest with one's self, and to decide to do surgery on one's self. I make the choice to cut myself for my own healing. The work at this level can be so intense that we think we are going to die, but we continue with the surgery anyhow. We have made the choice to endure the pain to be free.

Letting Go Is a Sojourn in the Valley of Indecision

The fourth stage of letting go is our sojourn in the valley of indecision. We are in the midst of surgery, and doubt creeps in. We are not sure that we will not die on the operating table. We are not sure that we can make it by ourselves. We are not sure that some love is not better than no love. We waver. We contemplate going back. We think about accepting violence and hate masquerading as love. Sometimes we spend a long time in the valley of indecision, and we cannot definitively decide. We go back and forth. One day we have ourselves together, and we declare, "This is toxic, and I'm letting go." The next day we are back in it, holding on and clutching harder than ever. It feels like one step forward and two steps back. We are in the valley of indecision.

There Is a Moment of Letting Go

The fifth stage of letting go is the moment of letting go. Little by little, we acknowledge that we are beyond the point at which we can return. We cannot always acknowledge the time and the place, but all of a sudden, quietly, from somewhere inside of us comes the resolve to give up trying to decide if it was a good decision or a bad decision. We decide that the decision has been made, and it is time to move on. The energy is not spent back in the past. The energy is spent making the most effective choices for a new future. The release has nothing to do with anybody telling us anything. The decision was made on the inside. It is time to let go, and we do.

What Tina Turner and the writer of Ecclesiastes did not say was, I believe the Holy Spirit directs this inner decision. The Holy Spirit is the power working in us that allows us to go through the process of letting go. The Holy Spirit is affecting the renewal of our spirits by helping us to let go. The Holy Spirit is deepening my sense of self. The Holy Spirit has me possessed of self. The Holy Spirit is giving me self-confidence. The Holy Spirit is filling me with self-respect. The Holy Spirit is causing me to exhale. The Holy Spirit is helping me to be self-evident. The Holy Spirit is giving me the right to make myself, to be myself, to explain myself, to love myself, to laugh with myself, to go to work for myself, to dream for myself, to cry for myself. But it would never happen if I didn't come to know that there is a time for letting go.

---

[1] Steve Duberry, "I Don't Wanna Fight," Chrysalis Music (ASCAP).

Study Questions

1. Dr. Thomas gives the example of a mother who gave all her savings to her wayward son. Are there some relationships that we cannot let go of? If so, how can we let go of negative influences and practices without letting go of the entire relationship?

2. Tina Turner said that she could not let go of an abusive marriage because of her own early life experiences of having been abandoned. Even though the marriage was destructive, she could not leave someone because of her unresolved pain over having been left. This insight demonstrates why we should not be so eager to judge whether people should leave relationships or stay in them. Discuss the difficulty of letting go experienced by those who themselves have been abandoned by others.

3. Dr. Thomas's analogy of the virus helps to shed light on why some people hurt other people. Does the knowledge that people who hurt others are virus-infected and therefore unable to regulate themselves help their victims to break away from them?

4. How can viewing the abuser as a virus help the victim to forgive him or her for the abuse?

5. What responsibility does a virus-infected person have to himself or herself and to others?

6. Read Philippians 3:13. Construct an example of letting go and apply the stages of letting go to that example.
   - Letting go hurts
   - Letting go means risking the loss of important things
   - Letting go means doing surgery on one's self
   - Letting go is a sojourn in the valley of indecision
   - There is a moment of letting go

Prayer Thought: O God, help me to know when it is time to let go.

Chapter Six

Help
and
Helplessness

1 Kings 21:5-7, NIV

And his wife Jezebel came in and asked him, "Why are you so sullen? Why won't you eat?"

He answered her, "Because I said to Naboth, the Jezreelite, 'Sell me your vineyard; or if you prefer, I will give you another vineyard in its place.' But he said, 'I will not give you my vineyard.' "

Jezebel his wife said, "Is this how you act as king over Israel? Get up and eat! Cheer up. I'll get you the vineyard of Naboth the Jezreelite."

His name was Ahab, and he fought back the only way he could. After all, open and obvious rebellion was not possible for one who was a crown prince. His father's name was Omri, and Omri was the king of Israel. Omri had purchased the hill of Samaria, founded and built a city upon it, and named that city Samaria. Yet Ahab heard whispers that his father did more evil in the sight of the Lord than all the kings of Israel before him had done. But how does one rebel when one's father is the king and one is the crown prince?

Ahab was not pleased with the relationship between his dad and himself, so he fought back the only way that he could. He could not openly rebel, but he could get low grades. He could not openly rebel, but he could be incompetent. He could not openly rebel, but he could hang out with the wrong crowd. He could not openly rebel, but he could play helpless and irresponsible.

Whatever came up, Ahab fought his dad with helplessness. He would crash the chariot and force his dad to bail him out. He would get caught drinking and drugging with several of his friends and force his dad to use political favors. He wanted to speak up for himself; he wanted to say what he thought, and what he wanted, and what he needed, but it is difficult to have a self in your parents' house if the parents won't allow it. He could not have himself. He could not be himself, and when you cannot have yourself or be yourself, you fight. Not all fighting is out in the open. Helplessness is a form of fighting.

He could not fight openly, but he could play helpless. He was so good at being helpless that he convinced everyone to conspire with him. They believed he was helpless and gave him a free ride because he was crown prince. He would get low grades, but since he was the prince, his teachers passed him anyhow. He would get in trouble with the police, but since he was the prince, the authorities favored him anyhow. He could play helpless, and he played helpless so long that the people began to treat him as if he were helpless.

In due time his father died, and even though the people believed the prince to be helpless, they were bound to make him their king. No different a king than a prince, he remained helpless with so little sense of self. But by the time he was crowned king, he had fought so hard and for so long that he became the act that he was playing. He became helpless, though he was once only playing helpless. When one plays and acts so long, one becomes the act. So he was helpless, and because he was helpless, he did what his father had done. He did more evil than did any of the kings that came before him. He even did more evil than his father, of whom it was said that he had done more evil than any of the kings before him.

Ahab married the foreigner Jezebel, daughter of Ethbaal, king of Tyre. Jezebel was a devotee of the Tyrean god Melqart, and she openly endorsed the worship of Baal in Israel. Because she openly endorsed the worship of Baal and because Ahab did not have a sense of himself, Ahab, the king of Israel, did likewise. Worse than that, he built a temple to Baal and blasphemed in front of the God of Israel. So Ahab provoked God.

The God of Israel sent the prophet Elijah to Israel to let Ahab know that God is God and that Baal *ain't* God. God put the word in the mouth of Elijah and said, "Go and say to Ahab that it will not rain until you say so. It is my authority to let it rain or not rain, but I give it to you. So if you say it will rain, it will rain. If you say it won't rain, it won't rain." Because of Ahab's sin, Elijah confronted Ahab and said, "So that you will know that God is God, it will not rain until I say so" (1 Kings 17:1).

It did not rain for three and a half years (1 Kings 18:1), and a famine swept the land. Ahab went home and told Jezebel what Elijah had said, so Jezebel decided to put to death the prophets of the Most High God. Elijah heard about the murder of the prophets and challenged Ahab to a confrontation on Mount Carmel. There, 450 prophets of Baal met Elijah, and they and Elijah each laid an ox on a pile of wood. The prophets of Baal called on their god to light fire to the wood, and Elijah called on the God of Israel to do the same. The god who lit the fire would be the real God. Elijah allowed the prophets of Baal to go first. He stepped into the background, and the prophets of Baal danced and sang and called on the name of their god, but no fire came down. They cut themselves, but no fire came down. Meanwhile, Elijah was in the background laughing and saying, "Why don't you sing a little louder? Is your god asleep?" Elijah was in the background making fun. After the prophets of Baal discovered that their god was not going to light the fire, Elijah stepped to the center stage (1 Kings 18:23-29).

Elijah said, "Bring some water, and pour it on that wood. Drench the wood, if you will, so that everybody will know that God is God." Then God rained down fire, and the fire not only burned up the wood but also soaked up the water, and it was clear that God is God. So the people bowed down and said, "The LORD—he is God!" (1 Kings 18:30-39).

Ahab went home and told Jezebel all that had transpired. Enraged at such an awesome display of God's power, Jezebel put the 450 prophets of Baal to death. Then she decided to put Elijah to death. She put out a contract on Elijah's life and vowed, "If the sun goes down tomorrow and I haven't killed you, may the gods deal with me" (1 Kings 19:2).

The Bible says that Elijah was nervous and ran into a cave. It is interesting that when Ahab was issuing threats, Elijah wasn't worried. But when Jezebel issued the threat, Elijah hid in a cave and told God that he wanted to die.

While Elijah was trying to work this thing out with God, the king of Aram mustered his entire army with thirty-two kings to attack Samaria. The king of Aram sent word to Ahab, saying, "This is what I want: your silver and your gold; they are mine. And the best of your wives and your children; they are mine." And you know what Ahab said? Ahab said, "They're all yours." Now that bothers me a little bit, for I would hope for a better response to such a demand than "They're yours." I would want the king to say, "We will fight to the death to defend our women, children, silver, and gold. In the name of the Lord our God, we will win." To send back a note and say, "They're all yours," is wimpish. And because the king of Aram and the thirty-two kings were viruses (and viruses replicate unless they're regulated), the kings sent back another note, saying, "Not only do we want the wives and the children, the gold and the silver; we want the palace and everything that you value" (1 Kings 20:1-6). When Ahab received the second message, he called a meeting of the elders of Israel and said, "I have received a letter, and these kings are looking for trouble" (1 Kings 20:7).

Why would the king call a meeting and say, "These kings are looking for trouble"? What an understatement. They were not looking for trouble. They were trying to take everything. Ahab was helpless, but more to the point, he had played helpless so long that he believed himself to be helpless. Accordingly, as king, he acted helpless. So the elders said, "Don't worry about this. Let's get together and let's at least fight." The elders offered the challenge. Then the Lord sent a prophet, and Ahab asked the prophet, "How are we going to do this?" The prophet, speaking for God, answered, "I am going to give you victory over the thirty-two kings, plus the king of Aram." Ahab replied to God, "But who is going to do it?" God said, "The young officers of the provincial commanders. They'll do it." Ahab asked, "Who will start the battle?" God responded, "You!" Ahab said, "Oh" (1 Kings 20:9-14).

Ahab went out and started the battle, and Israel's provincial commanders won. The Bible says that after the king of Aram and the allied forces were thoroughly defeated, they waited a year, gathered together again, and came back to fight some more. And God specified to Ahab, "Don't form a treaty with these folks; I am going to take care of them." The Bible says that after God allowed Israel's provincial commanders to beat them a second time, the king of Aram sought peace with Ahab, and Ahab, disobeying God's command, formed a treaty with him (1 Kings 20:32-34). Once again God sent a prophet to Ahab. Once again the prophet was livid and confronted Ahab, telling him to be careful, for his sin was about to catch up with him.

This background of Ahab's helpless nature brings us to our text. Naboth has a vineyard that is close to Ahab's palace. One day Ahab looks down from a window and wants to use the vineyard as a vegetable garden. He offers to give Naboth a better vineyard or to pay whatever Naboth thinks it is worth. But Naboth replies, "My daddy gave me this land, and I am not going to sell it. It is my family's land, and there is no price you can give me for it" (1 Kings 21:1-4).

Ahab says, "But I will give you a choice: beachfront property for this little garden."

Naboth replies, "I don't want beachfront property. This is my daddy's land. This is my people's land. So, no, we *ain't* selling it!"

The Bible says that in response to this, Ahab goes home, lies down on his bed, and sulks, refusing even to eat. Jezebel comes in, sees him sulking, and says, "Why won't you eat?" He explains the situation to her. Jezebel's outraged response is, "What kind of wimp are you? Aren't you supposed to be the king of Israel? I mean, get up! Cheer up! Get up off that helpless bed! Get up" (1 Kings 21:7).

And then the Bible says that Jezebel pushes the issue of help and helplessness one step further. She says, in essence, "If you won't work, I will get you a job. If you can't get the vineyard, I will deliver it to you." So Jezebel writes a letter under the king's signature, calling for a day of fasting and prayer, and puts Naboth on trial. She arranges for two false witnesses to testify that Naboth has blasphemed God and cursed the king. The sentence for such offenses is death, so Naboth is stoned to death. Word of his death is sent to Jezebel, who in turn says to Ahab, "Now rise. Get up. Go and take your garden" (1 Kings 21:9-16).

Help and helplessness. I am asking, What is help, and what is helplessness? What is real help, and when does help contribute to someone's helplessness? I am worried that much of the help we give people is no help. Let's consider four lessons concerning help and helplessness.

Helplessness Is an Act

For many, if not most people, helplessness is an act. Helplessness is a way to fight when the relationship system will not permit the expression of one's self. Many people are going around acting like they can't keep a job, acting like they can't run their lives, acting like they can't pay their own bills, all in an attempt to fight back. There are women who act like they can't live without a man. There are women who act like they can't live on their own. There are women who act like some piece of man is better than no man. There are women who act like Jezebel. If the brother is lying around and won't get a job, they go get one for him. If the brother won't be a man, they try to make him one or make up for his not being one. There are men who act like they cannot stop drinking. There are men who act like they cannot stop chasing women. Helpless, they cannot stop having affairs. Helpless, they cannot get a job. There are people who present themselves as helpless.

Helplessness is an act of a person who refuses to take any personal responsibility and who was probably reared in a family system that did not help him or her to develop a sense of self. Helplessness, for the majority who employ it, is an act, and sometimes they act it out so long that they become what they're acting out, believing themselves to be helpless.

Helplessness Has Many Forms

Helplessness has many forms. When one stops believing the helpless act and treats the helpless person like a responsible person, then helplessness mutates into other forms. One mutation is the con game. People who con other people are helpless people who have concluded that they cannot make it the straight and responsible way, so they run a game, a con, a scheme. Con games that are based in deviousness, outright deception, and manipulation are nothing but mutated forms of helplessness.

Another form of helplessness is the entitled complainer. People who exercise this form of helplessness think that life owes them something, so when they discover that they have to work for everything they get, they complain. Entitlement is laziness masked as privilege. Entitlement is the avoidance of the natural work that it takes for us all to live in this world. Many avoid the natural work by taking from those who have done the work. They justify stealing with their sense of entitlement. Some wait for their neighbor to go to work, and because they think they are entitled to whatever they want, they will break in while their neighbor is at work and take it. Entitlement is nothing but a mutated form of helplessness. Entitlement is laziness masked as privilege.

The chronically contentious express another mutated form of helplessness. The chronically contentious are folks who are always contentious. The function of contentiousness is to avoid the real issue that they are irresponsible. Contentiousness is a smoke screen that they use to bargain with the family. They will be less contentious if the family doesn't bring up any subject that will get them upset. Of course, what gets them upset the most is if someone wants to discuss their lack of responsibility. If the family breaks this unspoken but understood bargain, the contentious one becomes a small-time terrorist and is allowed to hold the entire family hostage; hence, no one can discuss the truth.

The same is true of the supersensitive. There are people who are so sensitive but at the same time so insensitive. Through their hypersensitivity, they attempt to force people to get caught up in their needs. People are so afraid to offend the supersensitive that they totally ignore their own needs, yielding to the needs of the supersensitive. As one of my major mentors said, "It is amazing how insensitive the sensitive are."

I am not saying that we should not help people. I am saying that we should help people from a perspective of self. We should not fall for the mutated forms of helplessness. Beware of the con game, the entitled complainer, the chronically contentious, and the supersensitive. Helplessness is an act of a person who refuses to take responsibility.

Helplessness Is a Form of Violence

Helplessness is a form of violence. We like to concentrate on the obvious and blatant forms of violence, such as slaps, verbal and psychological abuse, rape, and murder. Somebody hit somebody. Somebody slapped somebody. Somebody called somebody out of his name. Somebody beat up somebody. But I want to suggest that more people are done in by passive, dependent, innocent, and charming folk than by outright acts of violence. The combination of passivity, dependency, innocence, and charm creates a dangerous package that is often hard to resist. I am suggesting that women experience a disproportionate number of health problems compared with men. Our medical and psychological health systems are flooded with women's health problems. The majority of these are not the results of physical and psychological abuse. Many are cancers, heart diseases, ovarian problems, and so on. I believe this is connected to the fact that these women are often associated with passive, dependent, innocent, and charming men. Women are tricked into taking responsibility for helpless men. More women are being done in by helpless men than by rapists, murderers, and abusers. Ahab was probably passive, dependent, innocent, and charming. And when we are in relationship with helplessness, if we are not careful, we will think we are experiencing love. But what does love have to do with it?

Helplessness Can Control the Relationship

Helplessness can control the relationship. Helpless people are always looking for somebody to take over for them so they do not have to bear responsibility. Typically, the preaching emphasis in this text is that Jezebel did in Ahab. Jezebel is usually perceived as the wicked woman behind the throne, who is manipulating and controlling and doing vicious things. Jezebel gets a bad rap, and for some good reasons, but Jezebel should get no more than her share of the bad rap. I wonder if Ahab was not controlling and manipulating the relationship to make her look evil so he could look innocent. I wonder if Ahab did *her* in. I wonder if Ahab was such a wimp that he could not do his own dirt, so he played passive and dependent while his wife rescued him and did the dirt. When it came down to it, he could say, "It was Jezebel." He could pretend to be innocent.

Jezebel gets a bad rap. Jezebel has been a symbol of controlling, take-charge women. Down through the years, such women have been called Jezebels, but I wonder if Jezebel was not tricked by an entitled complainer, a chronically contentious, supersensitive con artist who was passive, dependent, innocent, and charming. I wonder if she was tricked into taking the heat while Ahab all the time was running things by being dependent. If we are not careful, the most dependent people in the family will be running the family, yet it will appear that the others are in charge. Helpless people have a way of being in charge of the whole family.

Help People from Our Position of Self

Help people from a position of knowing where our lines and limits are. We understand that we cannot take over for them; we cannot run their lives; we cannot control them for their own good; we cannot make good on their irresponsibility. If a man will not go to work, nobody can get him a job and make him go to work. We cannot make anybody do anything. We cannot make anybody stop doing anything. The only choice we have is to accept others' decisions and decide what we are going to do with our lives.

We should help, but with definite limits. We need limits because, if we are not careful, viruses will swallow us up. They will have us writing all of their term papers for their degree. They will have us doing all the work, then singing our sad refrain: "All these years, I put you through law school, and now you have left and gotten somebody new. I wrote all of those papers, and I did all of this, and I did all of that. I stayed up until four in the morning while you were sleeping, typing your papers." We will write some sad, victim-based love song and sell millions of copies because so many people identify and share a similar experience. But when we establish limits we understand that if somebody will not stay up for himself or herself, then we ought not to be up. With limits we understand that if a man will not work, he ought not eat. Why are you paying his rent and car note? We need limits. Help people from a position of self. Helpless people and helplessness will take over your self.

Look at God in verse 17. God is not fooled by the helpless game. The Bible says that Jezebel comes home and says to Ahab, "Now go down there and take the land." The Bible says that Ahab gets up off his bed, goes down in the garden to possess the land, and just as he's feeling good about finally owning it, God drops the prophet Elijah into the equation. Elijah confronts Ahab in the garden of Naboth and says, "You have murdered a man. *You* have. Not Jezebel. *You* have. *You* have done this thing. *You* have done what is wrong. *You* have. And because *you* have, dogs will lick your blood."

God is not fooled by the helpless game. God comes to the principal and says, "It's what *you* have done, and this is *your* sentence for *your* crime." And on the way to sentencing, God also mentions a sentence for Jezebel, so she doesn't get away scot-free. But God is talking to Ahab.

Yes, we have a God of grace and mercy; yes, we have a God of love, but sometimes the God of grace, and the God of mercy, and the God of love will become the God of judgment, and get in one's face, and not allow us to play helpless but will confront us about our behavior.

And the Bible says that when Ahab was confronted with his behavior, he repented in sackcloth and in ashes. When God put a limit on his helplessness . . . when God would not allow him to be a con man . . . when God would not allow him to be devious . . . when God would not allow him to be manipulative . . . when God would not allow him to be supersensitive, lying on the bed saying he couldn't eat because he couldn't have Naboth's land . . . when God would not allow him to be chronically contentious . . . when God said, "No. I'm going to deal with you on the basis of your being a mature adult who knew what you were doing," the Bible says that he repented in sackcloth and in ashes. He tore his clothes and repented. I wonder if it helps persons to repent when someone no longer believes their helpless act. God did not buy the helplessness, and Ahab repented.

Was Ahab's repentance a false repentance? Was it the kind of repentance that occurs only because a person is caught doing wrong? Well, at the close of the twentieth chapter, *God* is impressed with Ahab's repentance, and *God* says, "I'll lighten the sentence because of Ahab's repentance." We cannot fool God with a false repentance.

I am asking about help and helplessness. I am asking *you*, Why can't you quit drinking? Why can't you quit drugging? Why can't you stop chasing women? Why can't you stop the affairs? I am asking *you*, Why can't you live by yourself if God would have that for you? Why can't you get that job? Why can't you score high on the ACT? Why can't you get in that college? Why can't you excel? Why can't you grow? Why can't you extend? Why can't you stretch? Why can't you overcome? Why can't you overcome depression? Why can't you get out of abusive relationships? Why can't you grow past your misery? Why can't you?

Helplessness is probably an act, and in your helplessness, sooner or later the God of Israel is going to confront you in the garden and will move past all of your excuses, all of your helplessness, all of your con games, all of your lies, all of your deviousness, all of your tricks, all of your manipulation, all of your negativity, all of your chronic stuff, and say, "*You* have done this thing. Stop blaming your mama. Stop blaming your daddy. *You* have done it. I know your daddy was a king, but *you* have done this thing. I know about Jezebel, but *you* have done this thing. I know about the church folk, but *you, you, you* have done this thing!"

If *you* will allow the truth of the Lord God to confront your condition . . . if you will quit being manipulative with God and lay your situation out and tell God the truth and repent in sackcloth and in ashes, then the God of Israel will lighten your load.

The God that I serve will bring light out of darkness and help out of helplessness. The God that I serve will raise you and lift you high. The God that I serve can lift you out of the bad relationship. The God that I serve can lift you out of drugs. The God that I serve can lift you out of chasing women and drinking and drugging. The God that I serve can lift you. God can lift you. God can lift you. The God that I serve can lift you. God can set you up on a high place. God can lift you up. God can lift you. I know what I am talking about. God has lifted me. I know what I am talking about. God brought me out of darkness into his marvelous light. God can lift you. God can put the pieces back together. God can put the family back together. God can put your relationship back together. God can put you back together. God can put your hope back together. God can put your dreams back together. God can put your degrees back together. A lot of folk have degrees, but the degrees are in pieces. God can put everything back together. Yes, he can. And when God does it, you will come running. When God does it, you won't have any problem being a tither. When God does it, no one will have to beg you to come to Bible class. When God does it, nobody will have to beg you to come to prayer meeting. Nobody will have to tell you because whatever time of day or night service is held, you will be found there because you will have discovered that there is nowhere else to go, for only God has the word of life.

Study Questions

1. Discuss Ahab's helplessness. Does this view of King Ahab change your opinion about Jezebel? If so, how do you see her now?

2. Dr. Thomas says that helplessness is an act that people assume when they refuse to take responsibility for themselves. It has many forms. Look at the forms. How does each one express an individual's failure to take responsibility?
   • the con artist
   • the entitled complainer
   • the chronically contentious
   • the supersensitive

3. How do helpless people control relationships?

4. What are some strategies for avoiding being used by helpless people?

5. Can you identify helpless tendencies in yourself? What are they?

6. Why is God's response to Ahab so powerful and so helpful: "You have done this thing"? What does it force Ahab to do? How can we similarly respond to people who are playing the helpless game?

Prayer Thought: I will look inwardly to uncover the Ahab and the Jezebel in me. I will try to face my responsibilities and help others to face theirs by not doing for them what they should do for themselves.

Chapter Seven

Not Far from the Kingdom

Mark 12:28-34, NIV

One of the teachers of the law came and heard them debating. Noticing that Jesus had given them a good answer, he asked him, "Of all the commandments, which is the most important?"

"The most important one," answered Jesus, "is this: 'Hear, O Israel, the Lord our God, the Lord is one. Love the Lord your God with all your heart and with all your soul and with all your mind and with all your strength.' The second is this: 'Love your neighbor as yourself.' There is no commandment greater than these."

"Well said, teacher," the man replied. "You are right in saying that God is one and there is no other but him. To love him with all your heart, with all your understanding and with all your strength, and to love your neighbor as yourself is more important than all burnt offerings and sacrifices."

When Jesus saw that he had answered wisely, he said to him, "You are not far from the kingdom of God."

Not far from the kingdom. Not far. Not very far at all. Somebody's real close to the kingdom. You're real close to a breakthrough. You're real close to your deliverance. You're right there. You're not far. I know you feel a long way off. You're not far. You're right there. You're right there on the verge. You're not far. You're not far from your deliverance. You're not far from your freedom.

Mark seems to suggest that the question from the teacher of the law was a sincere question. Jesus had been teaching and answering questions in a debate, and a teacher of the law was impressed by the wisdom Jesus imparted in the discussion of each subject. The rabbis counted 613 individual statutes in the law: 365 that were negative and 248 that were positive. Rather than try to figure out 613 statutes, the studious rabbis attempted to formulate a few guiding principles from which the rest of the immense law could be deduced. And so, the sincere teacher of the law asked Jesus, "Of all 613 commandments, which one is the most important?"

In a similar vein, a Gentile challenged the great Jewish rabbi, Hillel, saying, "I'll convert if you can teach me the whole law while I stand on one foot." In other words, the Gentile was saying, "You have so many laws and so many regulations that you'll never be able to teach them to me before I get tired, so just tell me the main points, no more time than what I could hear while I stand on one foot." Hillel replied, "What you hate for yourself, do not do to your neighbor." This is the whole law. The rest is commentary. Go and learn. An honest look at how you want to be treated will provide important indicators on how to treat your neighbor.

Like Rabbi Hillel, Jesus does not hesitate to respond to the question of the teacher of the law. He quotes two passages from the Old Testament: Deuteronomy 6:4-9 and Leviticus 19:18. Deuteronomy 6:4-9 comprises the Shema that is recited by pious Jews every morning and every evening. The Shema goes like this: "Hear, O Israel. The Lord our God, the Lord is one." In the morning you can hear Jews saying, "Hear, O Israel. The Lord our God, the Lord is one." At night you can hear Jews saying, "Hear, O Israel. The Lord our God, the Lord is one." The Shema has been fundamental because it affirms three things that are critical to the Jewish faith.

First, the Shema affirms the unity of God. The Lord is unity. The Lord is whole. The Lord is one, not many gods, not broken down into a pantheon that we have to please, but the Lord is one God. Second, the

Shema affirms God's covenant relationship with the Jewish people. The Shema says, "The Lord, *our* God. The Lord has established a covenant relationship with the people. Third, the Shema affirms God's desire that Israel reciprocate the covenant love.

In the covenant, God gives God's love to the people; therefore, God expects the people to give themselves totally—heart, soul, strength, and mind—in love back to God. Jesus brings together Deuteronomy 6:5 and Leviticus 19:18 to show that the love of one's neighbor is a natural and a logical outgrowth of one's love of God. These commandments belong together. The teacher of the law had asked for the one most important commandment, and Jesus gave him two that were one. Jesus said, "You must love God and love your neighbor as you love yourself." There is absolutely no way that you can love God and not love your neighbor. There is no way that you can love your neighbor without loving yourself, and no way that you can love yourself without loving God first. Think on these things, and you will not be far from the kingdom of God. Contemplate and pray on these things, and you will not be far from that breakthrough that you've been looking for. Think on these things, and you will not be far from the deliverance you've desired. You are not far from the kingdom.

The first part of Jesus' response (Deuteronomy 6:4) is not so difficult for us to understand: to love God, to give one's whole self to God, to build a relationship with God, to hang out with God, to make God the most important aspect in one's life, to make one's relationship to God the most important thing in life. So when the text says, "Love the Lord your God with all your heart, and all your strength, and all your soul, and all your mind," it has a familiar ring because it has been embedded in a lot of us to love God with all our hearts, all our souls, and all our minds.

The second part of Jesus' response (Leviticus 19:18) is also familiar to us. Many of us have been taught from the time we could remember to love our neighbor. Almost any good Sunday school class or training union is going to instill this as a fundamental value. It has been deeply embedded in many of us to love our neighbor.

It is the third part of Jesus' response that I believe has received less attention and that we have more difficulty with. The "love our neighbor as ourselves" part throws us because we haven't quite grasped that it's OK to love ourselves; it's OK to like ourselves; it's OK to watch out for ourselves; it's OK to take the day off for ourselves; it's OK to live our lives for ourselves. In preparation for this sermon, I ran a reference check on the word *self*. The use of the word *self* in the Bible is overwhelmingly negative, denoting *selfish*. That's not what I'm talking about. I am talking about *self*. The Bible says that you can't love anybody if you don't love yourself. The Bible says that you can't take care of anybody if you can't take care of yourself. You can't encourage anybody if you can't encourage yourself.

One of the things that many of us do is go back and look at our family of origin. We go back and look at the house that we grew up in, and we think about what we did not have and what we did not receive, and we concentrate on that. Many of us would say that we did not receive all the love or attention that we wanted or needed when we were growing up. And some of us would say that we still do not receive what we think we need from our significant others. We're not getting all the love we want. We're not getting all the attention we want. We focus on deficiencies. Nobody told us that they were proud of us, or we didn't get very much encouragement. We focus on what we didn't have, what we missed. Nobody loved us. Nobody gave us the attention. We missed something, and then we leap from the past to the present and assume that if we'd had more love, we'd be able better to handle the problems that we have now. So we are looking for love and attention. We're trying to find love because we think that when we find it, we'll feel better and we'll function better. I might be wrong, but I want to suggest that the more we concentrate on what we did not get or did not receive, the needier we become. So the more unloved we feel, the more we need love.

People who feel unloved need more love. And the more unloved one feels, then the more love or attention one is wanting or needing. I might want to suggest that people who need love might be addicted to love. What I'm suggesting is that the more you connect love to what you didn't get when you were growing up, or what you didn't get in your last relationship, or what you didn't get and what you ain't never got, the more you need love. And the more you need love, the more you are addicted to love. And anything that has the word *addiction* connected to it sooner or later is going to end up in abuse.

When we focus on the love that we did not get, we become in the worst sense of the word selfish. When we focus on what we did not get, it can become justification to become spoiled, selfish, self-absorbed, and miserably self-indulgent. It becomes about what I can get, keep, and hoard for myself. Some of us are incredibly selfish, but I wonder if at the root of selfishness people don't justify it based upon the love and attention they did not receive.

What if we stop focusing on the love that we did not get? What if we stop focusing on what we thought we needed and did not get? What if we stopped looking at the deficiency in our bank account of love? What if we stopped focusing on what our parents did not do, what our spouse is not doing? What if we just learn to love ourselves? What if we made friends with the fact that suffering and lack are a part of life in this world and there may be some things that we will never have? What if we accepted the fact that some things we desire may never happen for us and that we'd better make the most of whatever we have and stop worrying about what we do not have? What if we accepted the fact that some things we deeply desire in our lives may never happen and then learn to love ourselves? What if we accepted the fragility of life and used the fragility to help us learn to love ourselves?

If our parents could have given us more love, they would have given it to us. They did the best they could with what they knew and what they understood. So what are you going to do? Are you going back to those childhood days and get the love you think they owe you? That is what many of us do: dream up some kind of fantasy love that will meet the need that has never been met before. We are looking for somebody to be what we have never had anybody to be.

We have a need, so we fantasize and make up a person to meet that need. Then we go around looking for somebody to drop our fantasy on. We're just looking for somebody to drop our love on. It ain't got nothing to do with the quality of the person involved. The person is not even close to the fantasy we created, but we need our fantasy. I wonder if your spouse would be a better spouse if you learned how to love yourself. I wonder if the church would be a better church if you learned how to love yourself. I wonder if your pastor would be a better pastor if you learned how to love yourself. It's amazing how wonderful people become in your life when you learn how to love yourself. When you learn how to love yourself, you're not needy, and when you're not needy you can put folk in proper perspective. You are not looking for somebody to be what nobody has ever been for you before.

What is love if you can't love yourself? What is love if you're looking for what you did not get when you were growing up? People who have not been loved don't need more love from outside people. I wonder if they need to love themselves. What if you took time to love yourself? What if you went on a long walk for yourself? What if you took a vacation for yourself? Laughed for yourself? Cried for yourself? Asked for some days off for yourself? What if every now and then you prayed for yourself? What if you encouraged yourself? What if you treated yourself? What if, instead of taking care of others all the time, every now and then you took care of yourself? Became a tither for yourself? Went to prayer meeting for yourself? Studied the Bible for yourself? Served God for yourself?

Maybe this is why we have to love the Lord our God with all our heart and all our soul and our entire being—because there is no love deficiency in the love of God. Though our parents could not love us with an everlasting love, though our spouse could not love us with an everlasting love, though our brothers and sisters could not love us with an everlasting love, God can love us with an everlasting love. When you get in relationship with God, you don't have love deficiency. God does not leave you unsatisfied. God can satisfy your soul with love. When you are in a love relationship with God, you don't go around being deficient, talking about what you didn't get, and what you did not receive, and what you still need. Somehow at the core of it all is to love the Lord your God with all your strength, and all your soul, and your entire mind. And when you love the Lord your God with all your strength, and all your soul, and your entire mind, you do not have a love deficiency, and so you're not going around needy, looking for somebody to be what nobody's ever been before to you. You already have all the love you need.

So what happens, brothers and sisters, is that in relationship with God you learn to love yourself. And when you learn to love yourself, you learn how to love your neighbor. When you learn to love yourself, you learn that people have the right to the same love for themselves that you have for yourself. When I appreciate my feelings and myself it helps me to appreciate others and their feelings because others have the same feelings and the same self. When I am not in deficiency, I can honor myself and give people the same honor that I give myself. But you cannot honor your neighbor if you cannot honor yourself. But you cannot honor yourself, if you do not honor God. You cannot love your neighbor if you do not love yourself, and you cannot love yourself if you do not love God.

When you get in love relationship with God, God doesn't leave you unsatisfied. It might not be the satisfaction you think you desire; it might not be the way you think you want it, but trust God in this thing, for I find that his satisfaction is all right with me. It wasn't what I thought I wanted, but I discovered that it was what I needed. It wasn't how I would have written the script, but when it works out, it's fine. It's just all right with me. Somebody said, "Jesus is just all right with me." The love relationship I have with God is just all right with me, and in my love relationship with God, I can love myself. In my love relationship with God, I feel good about myself. In my love relationship with God, I am confident about myself. In my love relationship with God, it's all right to take a vacation every now and then from work for myself, to quit every now and then for myself, to state my opinion for myself, to give for myself, to get some for myself, to pray for myself. It's paradoxical, but the more I love myself, the more I am in a position to love others. I have learned in ministry that the more rested I am, the more available I am to help people. The more I love myself, the more I allow others to love themselves.

A few years ago, I flew on a brand-new 757 out of O'Hare. I was flying to preach somewhere, and for the first time, I decided to pay attention to the safety demonstration that is given at the beginning of the flight. Normally I ignore the safety talk, but I paid attention this time because the presentation was given on pop-down video screens instead of by a flight attendant. When the part came where the oxygen mask falls down, I expected to hear, "If you have kids, put theirs on first." Instead what was said was, "Put your own oxygen mask on first." And I thought about that thing. You would think that if you have children what you're supposed to do is forego yourself and put theirs on first, but when I thought about it, I knew the video was right. You can't help anybody if you can't help yourself, and you can't bless anybody if you can't bless yourself. If you don't know God, how are you going to talk about God? You've got to get yourself straight. You can't love anybody if you don't love yourself. How are you going to help them when you can't help yourself? How are you going to show somebody the right way when you aren't traveling it yourself? How are you going to help somebody come off drugs when you aren't off them yourself?

I believe that there are some folk who are not far from the kingdom right here, right now. I believe there are some folk who can bear witness to what I am talking about, for they are witnesses to the love of God and how God can build self. They are witnesses to how God can lift you up out of the miry clay; how God can set your feet on a street called Straight; how God can turn your life around; how God can lift you up out of drugs; how God can get you out of beds you've got no business being in; how God can deliver you from a gambling table; how God can free you of your ego problem; how God can heal you of your difficulties in relationship. And God can establish you with a self. God will let you love yourself.

I believe there are witnesses who will tell Jesus, "Jesus, you're right about this thing." I believe that people will tell Jesus, "Yeah, Jesus, I believe I ought to love the Lord my God with all my heart, and all my soul, and all my mind, and then love my neighbor as myself," and Jesus sweeps through the house and says, "You're not far from the kingdom." You're real close right now. The church is on the verge of a Holy Ghost explosion right now. Something is about to break out. Something very God is about to break out. We're real close. We're not far. We're not far from the kingdom. We're not far from our deliverance. We are not far from our blessing. We are not far from our hope. We are not far from our strength. We are not far from this thing being real in our lives. We're not far. We are not far from having such an experience with God that we will have to veil our faces, so rich is the glow of God's glory. Somebody's not far today. Somebody's real close.

Study Questions

1. Jesus says the most important aspect of one's life is to make one's relationship to God the most essential thing in life. How does one go about doing this?
2. How does love for God help one to love oneself?
3. How does one go about loving oneself, especially if one feels unloved or in need of love?
4. Why, according to Dr. Thomas, is it so necessary for one to learn to love oneself?
5. If we love ourselves well, then what role does the love of others play in our lives?
6. How does self-love improve our love for others?

Prayer Thought: I will seek to love God first, asking God to teach me to love myself and others.

Chapter Eight

My Baby Daddy

Genesis 29:31-35, NIV

When the LORD saw that Leah was not loved, he opened her womb, but Rachel was barren. Leah became pregnant and gave birth to a son. She named him Reuben, for she said, "It is because the LORD has seen my misery. Surely my husband will love me now."

She conceived again, and when she gave birth to a son she said, "Because the LORD heard that I am not loved he gave me this one too." So she named him Simeon.

Again she conceived, and when she gave birth to a son she said, "Now at last my husband will become attached to me, because I have borne him three sons." So he was named Levi.

She conceived again, and when she gave birth to a son she said, "This time I will praise the LORD." So she named him Judah. Then she stopped having children.

Just my baby daddy. Yeah. He ain't nobody."
I knew from the first time that I saw this video, "My Baby Daddy,"[1] by B-Rock and the Bizz, that I would preach it. The phrase "my baby daddy" says tons and volumes, even as the voice of the young girl is crafted carefully to suggest her age, her maturity, or her lack thereof.

The male asking the question, "Who dat is?" raises the question as to whether or not he could be employed at IBM or Xerox. And so this video raises questions about the teens' resources to rear a family.

I want to talk to women about something I call a reproductive strategy. We read in Genesis 27 that Jacob's mother, Rebekah, schemed to trick his father, Isaac, and his brother, Esau, out of Esau's birthright. Jacob's name means "trickster," and he cooperated with his mother to manipulate his father, Isaac, and steal the birthright of his older brother, Esau. Esau was hairy, so Rebekah had Jacob put on a hairy fleece. He went in to his father, Isaac, whose sight was dim, and received his older brother's birthright. When Esau found out that his birthright was gone, he became angry. Seeing that the older brother might harm the younger brother, mother Rebekah sent Jacob to her brother Laban for safety.

When Jacob got to Uncle Laban's neighborhood among the eastern peoples, he ran into shepherds at a watering hole and said, "Do y'all know Laban, Nahor's grandson?"

They said, "Yeah."

"Is he doing well?"

They said, "Yeah."

It just so happened that Laban's younger daughter, Rachel, a shepherdess, was coming up the way with the sheep while Jacob was at a watering hole. There was a big stone that had to be moved at the watering hole, and it took many men to move it, but when Jacob looked at Rachel and saw how beautiful and lovely she was, the Bible says that he moved the stone by himself!

From the standpoint of beauty and physique, Rachel was "laying on full." The Bible says she was lovely of form and pleasing to the eye. She took Jacob to meet her father, his Uncle Laban, who had two daughters, of whom Leah was the elder. The Bible says that Leah had a weak eye, which means she had something that detracted from her appearance, but the younger Rachel was lovely of form and fair to look at.

Jacob fell in love with Rachel, but he had come to Laban empty-handed and had no bride price, no dowry, so if he was going to get

Rachel, he had to give up something. He offered himself in service for seven years of labor so he could have the hand of Rachel in marriage. Rachel was so beautiful and so attractive that the Bible says even seven years did not seem a long time to Jacob.

Remember, Jacob's name means "trickster" or "deceiver," but Laban was quite a trickster himself. When the time came for Rachel to marry Jacob, Laban put together a big wedding feast to which the bride came veiled. Jacob had worked seven years for this moment, but when he woke up the morning after the wedding night and the bride removed her veil, he discovered that he had Leah and not Rachel. Naturally he was upset and went to his uncle, who said, "I can't give away the younger one before I give away the older one." (You see the same trick was being played on Jacob that he had played on his father, Isaac, and brother, Esau, when he tricked his older brother out of the birthright.) So Laban says, "Keep Leah. Work seven more years, and you can have Rachel." However, Laban allowed Jacob to marry Rachel after Jacob observed the customary first week's marriage rites and festivals with Leah. So he had Rachel after a week, but on credit; he still had to work for his father-in-law for seven more years to pay for her (Genesis 29:25-30).

At this point, the Bible says a very hurting thing: Jacob loved Rachel more than he loved Leah (Genesis 29:30). When somebody you love, loves someone else more than you, it's a hurting thing. The Bible says, "When the LORD saw that Leah was not loved, he opened her womb, but Rachel was barren" (29:31). The Lord opened up Leah's womb and gave her a son, and so she said, "Surely my husband will love me now" (29:32). Jacob did not love her and did not want her, for his eye was on Rachel. Somebody knows what I am talking about when I say that he slept with her, but he did not really want her; though they had sex together and children together, he really did not love her. Somebody asked Leah of Jacob, "Who dat is?" and Leah replied, "He ain't nobody. Just my baby daddy." In other words, nothing's going on. No deep love. No deep relationship. Just my baby daddy. "We have sex, yeah, but he's just my baby daddy."

I want to explore how we go from making love to "He ain't nobody.

Just my baby daddy." I am assuming that when people get together and have sex, there is love in the equation, and some hopes and some dreams are involved. Therefore, I wonder how the male goes from her love partner to nobody. How does he go from being considered a worthy partner to "just my baby daddy"? I am interested in that gap. I am concerned about that distance: how somebody goes from being a sex partner that you have hopes and dreams with to being *just* my baby's daddy.

We must understand that the backdrop of this text portrays a very male-dominated culture. Women were considered as property, and women had few rights men were bound to respect. Women were given as a business deal between one man and another, usually the father and the prospective son-in-law. The young man would have to pay the daddy for the right and privilege to marry the daughter, and according to this custom, the girl was just a chip in the deal based upon her beauty and childbearing ability. This is a text about Jacob and Laban, and the women in the text are incidental except for their physical appearance and childbearing potential. It's a business deal.

Let's take love out of the equation of these relationships for a few minutes. One of the signs of maturity is to be able to separate romance, love, sex, and reproduction. Romance, love, sex, and reproduction are four distinct and different stages of relationship, requiring increasing levels of commitment and sophistication. One progresses from one stage to the next only with time and the successful completion of the commitments of that phase. Women who do not allow time and the successful completion of each appropriate phase run all the phases together too quickly and end up in spiritual, physical, and emotional trouble. Love is the excuse we use to speed things up when we move from romance to reproduction without necessary time and caution, as is the case in the video.

Let's take love out of this equation. Let's separate love from sex. When we take love out of sex, then what we have is a business deal. In a good business deal, you trade something of value—a product, a good, or a service—and you get a product, a good, or a service of equal value in return. The most valuable product, good, or service women have is sexual access and favor. This is not all women have, but it is one of the things that they have that many men value the most. *Therefore, one of the most essential questions a woman must answer is what she will trade for access to her sexuality and favor.* In other words, what kind of business deal will she negotiate with a man to allow him sexual access and favor? What you trade yourself for has to do with how much you value yourself, and we don't like to admit it, but some high-level negotiations are going on between men and women. Because we don't like to admit that, we use the concept of love to cover up the negotiation, or we ignore the fact that we are engaged in trading something of the highest value. That's why we have all these videos about love. Love this and love that, just covering up the negotiations going on between a man and a woman.

Negotiations between the sexes in adolescence or early adulthood are tremendously complicated. Negotiations between grown folks are complicated, but especially between young people as represented in the "baby daddy" video. Usually both sexes are inexperienced, and both parties have an imperfect understanding of the value of what they are trading. This is especially problematic for a young woman because if she signs on a bad business deal, she can often end up with a child or a lifetime of parenting or emotional scars, or if she is a single parent, a reduction of her value on the open market since many men are less likely to invest in someone else's children. A lot of us brothers are trying to get notches on our belts; we are just having sex, but a woman is doing something beyond that, and so she expects that she is getting something fair in return. She is trading herself, but when she gets nothing in return, either she has to do violence or she has to distance herself by limiting her emotions and saying, "He ain't nobody. Just my baby daddy." Many young women today are at risk for a bad deal because of three factors that I see in this text. Many women misperceive three things.

Women Misperceive Their Sexual Value

First, women misperceive the great value of their sexuality. In our text, Jacob and Laban understand the price of Rachel's sexuality. Jacob says,

"I will work for seven years." Jacob and Laban understand that *women control the ultimate resource, which is access to a woman's reproductive future.* Jacob and Laban understand that a man can't carry on the lineage without a woman. So access to a woman's reproductive future is more valuable than a million dollars. But women don't know this. Maybe Leah understands some of this because she says, "Maybe now he will love me. Maybe now that I have allowed his lineage to continue, he'll appreciate me." She understands some of that, but in the culture in which she operated, women were not allowed to use the value of their sexuality for their own benefit. It was more for the daddy's and the husband's benefit. I wonder how many women in today's culture understand the full value of their sexuality.

Women Misperceive Their Level of Maturity

Second, many women misperceive their own developmental (emotional, physical, and spiritual) maturity to enter negotiations for sex. The younger a woman is, the more attractive she is and the more negotiating power she has in regard to sexual access. The older a woman becomes, the less desirable she is to many men, who, for the most part, seem to value firm bodies and young looks. Paradoxically, at the time that a woman is most desirable to the wider population of men, which means she has the most control over her sexual resource, she is usually not yet mature enough to handle her most valuable asset. At the time when her sexual access and favor are the most valuable she is too developmentally immature to handle these assets. Many young women think that they are ready to handle their assets, but they misperceive their developmental—physical, spiritual, and emotional—maturity.

The young girl on the videotape misperceives her developmental maturity. She thinks she's ready. But when you listen to her, her immature voice suggests that she is not ready to be dealing with what men consider to be her most valuable asset and resource. Many women misperceive the great value of their sexuality. Many women misperceive their developmental maturity. This is a flaw in the reproductive strategy of many women that hinders them from obtaining the full benefit of their resources.

Women Do Not See Themselves as Equals

Third, many women do not perceive themselves as equals in the midst of a culture that sees them as less. Rachel and Leah knew they were slated in the culture for lower status than men had. Many women today also know, quite intuitively, that they are slated for less and are valued less in this culture than are men. Many women come from families where females have little power and males may be valued more. If a girl watches this long enough, she perceives herself to have relatively low status. Psychopathology or low self-esteem may develop; neurosis or a lack of self may develop, which causes an inhibition or a failure to develop or utilize personal strengths. All daughters are attractive, but if they have been devalued in the home they may strike a poor bargain with a young man. Many women do not perceive themselves as equals in the midst of a culture and a home that see them as less.

When you go into a business deal and you misperceive yourself or the value of yourself, you will not get fair value. And girls and young women, and many older women, are giving away sexual favor for extremely low value. Many are allowing sexual access and favor and not getting a doggoned thing in return. No marriage license. Just giving up sex. Move in, clean house, cook, no marriage license, just access and favor. Just giving away their most valuable asset, just having babies for men. Just giving sexual access on some vague, indescribable, and untested concept called love. What's love got to do with it?

Tina Turner was right. What does love have to do with it? What does love have to do with how you value yourself, how you respect yourself, how you negotiate for yourself? Love is separate and distinct from that. I mean, he has no job? I mean, he offers no insurance? I mean, *a* baby has to have *the* baby on the parents' insurance? He has no resources and ultimately no commitment.

He goes from the bedroom to "just my baby daddy" because she has traded herself and gotten nothing in return. He promises her love but delivers very little, and to handle the hurt and pain of the unfair exchange, she must distance herself. But she can't distance herself totally because they have a child together, so she banishes him to the fringe of her life: "He ain't nobody; just my baby daddy." And it hurts even more because when she gets ready for a new business deal, the next guy in negotiations wants to see who else has had sexual access: "Who dat is?" he asks. "What kind of relationship y'all got? Who dat is keep calling here?"

"That ain't nobody. Just my baby daddy."

But the new partner is suspicious because he recognizes there was a business deal going on and wonders about her value. Her present value is diminished because of the bad deal she has to continue to be involved in, at some level.

"Who dat is?"

"Just my baby daddy."

But despite our bad business deals, there is a God. This text says when *God* saw that Leah was not loved . . . when *God* saw that she had been used as a pawn . . . when *God* saw that she had been manipulated . . . when *God* saw that she was just a chip being used in a deal . . . when *God* saw that she was just being thrown back and forth . . . when *God* saw. The first place to start, women, is in a relationship with God. *God should be your primary resource.* You ought to be in Bible class to meet God. You ought to be in a small group to get God, to see God. You ought to have a devotional life to be with God. You ought to be a tither to express your appreciation to God, because when you are not loved, there's nothing any man can do for you. It starts with God. You can't guarantee that the man is going to stay, so you'd better get in relationship with God. You can't guarantee, as you get older, that he might not walk around with a younger body, so you'd better get in relationship with God. *When God saw.*

God Will Teach You the Value of Your Sexuality

First, I believe when you get in relationship with God, God will teach you the great value of your sexuality. God will teach you that God made you a gifted woman, intelligent, smart, wise, beautiful, and with a precious gift of reproductive capacity. God will teach you that this is not all you have, but it is a valuable resource, and God will teach you and show you how to value it, how to use it, when to use it, and whom to use it with. God will show you. God will teach you the great value of your sexuality.

God Will Help You to Mature

Second, God will help you with your developmental immaturity. God will help you to discern the proper time to use your great asset, based upon the Word. God will let you know when it's not time yet because you're too young, because you're too undeveloped, because you don't have a license and a measure of legal security. No, don't move in with the man yet. He doesn't want to marry you. Don't give up sexual access and favor. Just don't lie down. Don't do that. No, no, no. You're not ready. You've got to stay with God for a little while so God can teach you who you are. God says, I've got to show you who you are. I've got to raise up your physical, your spiritual, and your emotional maturity. I've got to get you ready before you can get in a business deal so you will have full value because with full value, even if he walks out, you've still got you.

God Will Raise Your Self-Perception

The third thing God will do is raise your status in your own eyes, regardless of how those around you value you. God will raise your own low perception of yourself. Jesus raised the status of so many women. There was a woman at the well (John 4). Jesus raised her status. See, it was not proper for rabbis to be seen talking to women in public, but there he was having a conversation, teaching this woman the Scriptures, opening up the Word of God to her. He raised her status. He raised her self-esteem. He showed her that she had made some bad reproductive strategy choices, but that was all right. He had some living water that would well up into everlasting life into her soul. He was raising her reproductive status strategy, her sense of herself. He was raising her self-esteem so that she would value herself. When he got through, she ran and told the townspeople, "There's a man in town. *A real man.* This one ain't trying to sleep with you. This one values you for you. This one told me about myself, told me who I was and what I was, told me the husbands that I had. He didn't judge me with the knowledge that he had. He offered me a new future."

When you allow God to teach you the great value of your sexuality . . . when you discern your developmental maturity . . . and when you raise your status in your own eyes, then you will be like Leah in verse 35. After giving birth to three sons and naming them with names that conveyed her grieving hope that her husband would love her, she gave birth a fourth time. Only this time she seemed to understand the great value of her sexuality. This time she seemed to discern her developmental maturity. This time she seemed to appreciate her status, so she said, "This time I will praise the Lord. Call the child Judah, for I will praise the Lord. I will no longer look to any man for validation and love. I will praise the Lord."

---

[1] "My Baby Daddy," Arista Records, Inc.

Study Questions

1. Leah, the unloved wife, could say only that Jacob was her babies' daddy. In the same way many women, particularly young women, become mothers without the benefit of a shared parental relationship with their babies' fathers. Dr. Thomas says that the notion of romantic love needs to be set aside long enough to allow a woman to discern whether or not she is receiving fair value for what she brings to a relationship. Discuss the concept and implications of her receiving fair value.

2. If we look at relationships as business deals that need to be negotiated, what things are important to sustain a love-based relationship? For a woman with a man? For a man with a woman?

3. What can parents and guardians and school, community, and church leaders do to help girls understand the great value of their sexuality?

4. How far do you think our culture has come in validating the equal worth of women to men? Are there ways in which women are still treated as second-class citizens? What are these? How can we address these issues?

5. The points in this sermon suggest a study course for women and girls. Perhaps some group in your church or community can structure seminars or classes around these topics.

- Women misperceive their sexual value
- Women misperceive their level of maturity
- Women do not see themselves as equals
- God will teach women the value of their sexuality
- God will help women to mature
- God will raise women's self-perception

Prayer Thought: Open our eyes, O God, that men and women will know the true worth of those whom you created as female, and help all women everywhere to receive fair value for their investment in love.

Chapter Nine

Baby Daddy

Genesis 27:30-34, NIV

After Isaac finished blessing him and Jacob had scarcely left his father's presence, his brother Esau came in from hunting. He too prepared some tasty food and brought it to his father. Then he said to him, "My father, sit up and eat some of my game, so that you may give me your blessing.

His father Isaac asked him, "Who are you?"

"I am your son," he answered, "your firstborn, Esau."

Isaac trembled violently and said, "Who was it, then, that hunted game and brought it to me? I ate it just before you came and I blessed him—and indeed he will be blessed!"

When Esau heard his father's words, he burst out with a loud and bitter cry and said to his father, "Bless me—me too, my father!"

It might be very healthy and mature to separate love, sex, romance, and reproduction. When we separate love from sex, then an aspect of the male and female relationship that usually is not apparent becomes crystal clear: the fact that the male and female relationship is a business deal.

In a good business deal, one gets a fair rate of exchange for a good, a service, or a product that one offers to another. Women must think about whether or not they are getting fair exchange for one of their most

89

important gifts: access to their reproductive futures and sexuality. I am suspicious that many women are exchanging themselves—giving up their sexuality—for virtually nothing in return, for some vague and uncommitted notion of love. And I ask, and I continue to ask, "What does love have to do with it?" Is love a reason to make a bad business deal? Is love a reason to give yourself to someone and get little or nothing in return? Is that love? Why do we call that love?

Women should begin to think about a reproductive strategy. A reproductive strategy involves a plan to receive fair exchange for access to one's sexuality and one's reproductive future. In turn, men need to do some thinking about their resource strategy.

You can see the bad business deal in the video "My Baby Daddy." It portrays a young woman who has no reproductive strategy. She is a teen mother who probably had sex based upon the fact that the baby's daddy promised love. You can tell from the squeaky, teen sound of her voice that she is not ready for the awesome responsibility of negotiating about her sexuality and the child that results from those negotiations. It is also clear from the video that Baby Daddy has no resource strategy, and he probably used the word *love* to get sex.

While we do not want to stereotype anyone, it is difficult to be gainfully employed in our culture, running around talking about "Who dat is?" The video is constructed with the young man saying, "Who dat is?" to represent youth and immaturity that is not ready to handle the awesome responsibility of sex and reproduction. In other words, we might have important indicators to the resource strategy of a young man when he is running around talking about "Who dat is?" The young woman needs a reproductive strategy, and the young man needs a resource strategy. We have a successful parenting effort when the female has a reproductive strategy and the male has a resource strategy. But in this video, neither one is operative.

A reproductive strategy and a resource strategy involve two things: number one, the mating effort, and number two, the parental effort. I think we have the mating effort down pretty well, so let's focus on the parental effort, which involves significant investment by the parents in such a way that the offspring has a chance to survive and develop into a mature and contributing member of society. A resource strategy is a plan to have resources that will allow one to provide for the mother and the child. A resource strategy is a plan to invest in an offspring and a family in such a way that the offspring's and the family's chance of survival and maturity are increased. A resource strategy does not stop because the father and the mother split up. A resource strategy runs independent of whether or not the couple is getting along. A resource strategy is a commitment and responsibility the moment you have sex with any woman, regardless of the long-term implications of the relationship.

God knew that you would not be ready for that level of commitment and responsibility for a long time, and that's why God prescribed sex within the context of marriage. God understood the heavy commitment of resources that are an automatic obligation the moment you have sex with any woman. The moment you have sex, you have a commitment to provide resources to her and the child if a child should be born. Like it or not, this is the level of commitment that is necessary if we would maturely handle our sexuality.

What I see is brothers having sex but no resource strategy. What I see is brothers indulging in the first stage of the reproductive strategy, the mating effort, but not developing a resource strategy. Sex, but no commitment and no responsibility. Just making babies. Just being Baby Daddy. Not close, not intimate, not involved, just Baby Daddy. Not an intimate relationship with a mother, just Baby Daddy. No commitment to the child. Just Baby Daddy. No lifelong commitment of resources. Just Baby Daddy.

Now, I do not want to paint all the brothers with the label of Baby Daddy. A brother said to me, "Pastor, you're right, but she won't let me see the baby." And I said, "Just because you and the mama have a bad business deal going doesn't mean it should affect the business deal with the child."

Another brother said, "Pastor, she don't want no help." Well, give her some anyhow. And if you have to take all the money and put it in a mutual fund that you give to the child at a later date, do that, for there are always ways to fulfill your responsibility. Stop using the mother as an excuse for why you are not providing a resource strategy. The moment you have sex with a woman, you are making a commitment to provide resources. All of this should be thought about before you lie down and have sex with somebody. Many of us don't think about this, though. We're just being Baby Daddy.

There was a mother in the Bible who knew the value of a resource strategy, and to make sure her son had one, she tried to provide it. Her name was Rebekah, and Rebekah was married to Isaac. They had two sons, Jacob and Esau. The Bible says that Jacob was her favorite. Already we know there's trouble. If you want to find trouble in any family, find out who the favorite one is, because if there's a favorite, there's a nonfavorite. If there's a favorite, that suggests there's an imbalance in the emotional system of the family because it ought to be that everybody and every child can be the favorite, that every child can get special treatment. Because Jacob was the favorite, Esau had to be the nonfavorite. The favorite one has an in-track to the family's resources, which means that somebody's left out and has an out-track to the family's resources. And that's just what happened in this family. Rebekah schemed to secure the inheritance of the older brother, Esau, for the younger brother, Jacob, her favorite.

Rebekah went to Jacob and said, "This is what we're going to do. We're going to fool your daddy, Isaac. He's an old man now, getting close to death, so the time has come for him to pass on the blessing. What you're to do is go out and catch his favorite game and bring it back for me to fix it up. Next, since your father does not see well and depends upon touch and smell, we're going to put hair on you so you will feel like your hairy brother, and we're going to dress you in one of Esau's garments so you will smell like him. Then you will take the meal in, and you'll be there to receive the blessing and the inheritance."

And this is what happened. If you read the text, you will discover that Isaac is not totally fooled, for he thinks he hears Jacob's voice, but the smell and the touch are Esau's, so thinking that Jacob is Esau, Isaac gives the blessing to Jacob (Genesis 27:23). In the meantime, just as Jacob leaves the tent, in comes Esau, who has gone hunting, killed his father's favorite game, and prepared it just the way his daddy likes it.

The Bible says that Esau walks in and says, "Now, daddy, I am ready to receive my blessing" (Genesis 27:31). And Isaac says, "Well, who are you? I already gave the blessing to Esau." And he says, "But I'm Esau." And then come those powerful words from Esau: "Bless me, too, my father. Hast thou no blessing for me?" (27:34,36). And Isaac responds, "The blessing is already gone. I have no blessing for you."

Is this the way to get resources? To steal someone else's inheritance? Is this the way to get resources? To engage other people in deceptive business deals and deceitful practices? Is this the way to get resources? To trick and deceive one's father and brother? Is this the way to get resources? To take somebody else's blessing? To trick and deceive somebody by selling drugs? To pimp and misuse women? Is this the way to get resources? To lay up on a woman without a job? To have a woman take care of you while you're trying to be an artist, or get in the movie business, or get your rap song to take off? Is this the way to get resources? To live off your mama or your daddy and your girlfriend, talking about "I'm my own man," and you aren't even paying your own bills? A man pays his own bills and takes care of his responsibility.

You're living with your girlfriend, living off your mama and daddy, letting mama and daddy take care of that grandchild that you ought to be taking care of because they cannot bear to see the child go hungry and go without. You're letting welfare take care of your children and even your wife, talking about "I'm my own man." Nobody ever gets anywhere by letting the government take care of his family. You're looking for fast money, playing horses, shooting dice, shooting pool, playing numbers, playing the dozens, playing the lotto, playing the casino, standing on the corner, drinking 40s, doing drugs, getting high, shucking and jiving, dodging and hiding, just being Baby Daddy.

Is this the way to get resources? To steal somebody else's blessing? To break into other people's houses while they're at work and take what they have, talking about white folks, "and they brought us here four hundred years ago and put us in slavery, and we ain't got no job today 'cause what white folk done done"? Is this the way to get resources? To put a ski mask on and stick up the 7-Eleven store? To wait in the parking lot at the grocery store and snatch some elderly woman's purse? To hide in the alley and put a gun to somebody's head and take his wallet? Just being Baby Daddy. No resource strategy. Just Baby Daddy. No intimate connection. Just Baby Daddy. No parental investment, just a sex machine. Just Baby Daddy. No resources to raise a family. Just Baby Daddy.

You cannot build your family on somebody else's blessing. You can't raise a family ducking and diving, shucking and jiving. You've got to have a resource strategy.

Most women know a large number of men who would be quite willing to have sex with them. The problem women face is finding a man of sufficiently high status and moral character who is willing to make a commitment and who has the necessary resources to be involved in the parental effort. Unlike women with their nearly unlimited choices of male sexual partners, only those men of relatively high status and position have a large range of potential female sexual partners. In other words, only men like professional athletes and actors, musical artists and rap stars have the range of potential sexual partners equal to that of females. Females are attracted to them, not necessarily because they're good looking, but because of their resource base. Women who run after superstars do not run after them because they are handsome brothers. A brother looks better when he has resources. Professional athletes look like a million dollars because they do have, in fact, a million dollars, and even more. So the average woman has the possibility of more sexual partners than does the average man, and when women find men who have tremendous resources, some of them literally throw themselves at the men. Stereotypically, these women are called groupies.

This analysis points to the fact that most men start with few mating opportunities and low status. Many men without significant resources, especially those who are young, have very low status and relatively few mating opportunities. Now somebody's going to argue that I am wrong about that because some men who are young and have low status have plenty of mating opportunities, *but that's only because the women don't understand their value.* Consider this. When women understand who they are, they control sexual access. They have the upper hand, and the man gives gifts and is chivalrous to prove his love so the door to sexual access will open for him. It is, most often, therefore, the attitude of the woman that controls sexual access. But if a woman doesn't know who she is or where she's going, or what her value is, or the value of her reproductive future, then she gives sex up, without appropriate resources and exchange.

Trickery and deceit are not effective plans for a resource strategy, either. In the text, when Esau realizes what has happened, he gets angry and wants to kill Jacob. It doesn't do any good to have an inheritance and then be killed. That's why selling drugs is a poor resource strategy. A drug seller wants to tell me, "I make more than you do." The drug dealer probably does make more than I do, but I might be around a little longer to enjoy what I have. You don't have any long-term future in deceit and trickery. Jacob has to run out of town and go to Uncle Laban's to escape the wrath of Esau. When Jacob gets to Uncle Laban's, he has nothing, but he wants Rachel. And guess what Uncle Laban says? What resource strategy do you have? What do you have to offer? What are you bringing to the table? I am not going to allow you sexual access to my daughter unless you can pay me. The conversation might have gone something like this:

"What do you have?"

"Well, I ain't got nothing."

"Well, what are you going to do?"

"Well, I'm going to work. I'm going to work seven years, and you set the income level."

Jacob was willing to work seven years with Laban setting the income level. Many brothers today say, "No, I'm not going to work no minimum-wage job; that's beneath me." Never mind that they do not have any skill or training that is marketable, and without skill and training all they will be able to get is a minimum-wage job. But like Jacob I say, "No, ain't nothing beneath me because I am on my way somewhere. I am a valuable and intelligent man, and if you put me in a $4.25 an hour job as a street sweeper, I am going to do such a good job that by the time my probationary period is up, I am going to get a raise. Before too long, I am going to do such a good job that they will make me a supervisor, then they will make me a manager, then a vice president, and when I finally learn the entire business, I will open up my own street-sweeping company." I am on my way somewhere. If I am not on my way anywhere, I cannot take a minimum-wage job because I am not going anywhere, and that is where I will end up. But you can take any job if you are on your way somewhere.

I believe that as churches all over the country we should instill in young and old men four components of an effective resource strategy: an income-producing strategy, a complementing partner strategy, a support strategy, and a relationship with God.

An Income-Producing Strategy

First, let's look at an income-producing strategy. If a young man is going to develop a resource base that is going to put him in a position to provide for a family, he must decide from one of four options:

He may go to trade school.
He may go to college and head in a professional direction.
He may open his own business.
He may work for a corporation and make sure it gives to the community.

Every young man needs to select one of these options, and it does not matter which one. Those who choose to become doctors should be considered no more valuable than those who become tradesmen. The community needs people in all four categories. Every young man ought to be prepared to pursue one of these options before he graduates from high school. Every young man needs to understand that if he is going to have a family, he has to have a resource strategy. The church must say to young men, "An income-producing job is part of a resource strategy, so choose one. We will help you, support you, and back you."

A Complementing Partner

Second, we must also tell young men that they need a complementing partner because God said that it is not good that a man should be alone. This does not mean that every man should marry, but if marriage is the choice, the relationship should be one of dignity and equality for both parties, or what I call a complementing partner. A complementing partnership is one with mutuality as the guiding light of the relationship. Mutuality is the belief that I can never be fully male until she is fully female. In other words, as she reaches and fulfills her highest potential, so will I fill mine. I am to encourage her to reach her highest and best because in doing so I am fulfilling the highest and best in myself. So you don't hold her back; you don't compete with her. You nurture her and grow her, develop her, and support her. In doing this for her, you do it for yourself.

For example, some men are afraid of a female who is a financial equal because money changes the dynamics in a relationship. Men have had an age-old trick of controlling women through the money, and once they get a partner who is able to outresource them financially, the dynamics change, and brothers have trouble because they don't know how to relate without that power position. When one truly sees the mate as a complementing partner, it is irrelevant who makes the money because it is about *we* and *us* and not always *me, my,* and *I.*

A Support Strategy

Then, third, a resource strategy involves a support strategy. A support strategy ensures that not all male support comes from women. I believe that men are so sexually dependent on women because men have not learned how to allow other men to minister to them and nurture them. Because the males in their lives are largely silent, men begin to fantasize about sex and what sex can accomplish. But a man who is grounded by other men and who is supported, prayed for, and loved by other men finds less need to be dependent on women for sex. If a man is getting no real support from the other men in his life and offering no support to the other men in his life, then when his heart hurts, he sits down in front of the tube and watches Halle Berry and wants her. He comes to his job, looks at a woman bending over at the water cooler, and decides that if he could just have that, he wouldn't hurt anymore.

Harold Washington was the first African American mayor of the city of Chicago. Harold Washington was on the verge of making Chicago government truly representative of all the people for the first time in the history of Chicago, but he tragically died of a heart attack. Harold Washington died at the average age that most black men die, sixty-four. As I reflected on the deep loss, I came to believe that a heart attack is a metaphor for the heart blowing up. Tears are the release valves of the heart, and when we do not cry, I wonder if we store the pain all up until finally our hearts explode. Of course, this is speculation, but what if we men could have other men that we could cry with, other men that we could speak the deep secrets and truth of our heart to? I wonder, if we had more release valves, would so many of our hearts explode?

A Relationship with God

Fourth, though it should be number one, every man ought to have a relationship with God. I've said it often. I'll say it again: A man without God is like a seed blowing on the wind. There's no telling where he's going to land. At the bottom of the resource strategy is a relationship with God, who indicates to me my value and my worth as a man . . . a God who indicates to me that I am valuable, that I am intelligent, that I am smart . . . a God who indicates to me that God's not going to leave me stuck in a $4.25 an hour job . . . a God who knows that I have or may want to have a family and will need resources. All I have to do is get out there and take the job, and the God I serve will help me grow and prosper. The God I serve lets me know who I am.

If I have a relationship with God, I don't have to run around, competing with my wife, scared that she's going to get an award or degree that I don't have . . . scared that she's more accomplished than I am. I don't have to be bothered with that. The God I serve will give me a support strategy, will show me brothers that I can tell the truth to and pray with, and brothers I don't have to be strong with all the time. I will see a woman bend over at the water cooler and be able to distinguish fantasy from reality. A relationship with God. A relationship to God. A relationship with God. You've got to have it. Brothers, you've got to know for yourself that one-on-one, personal, intimate relationship with God. That's ultimately what I'm offering. I'm offering God. I'm offering a huge dose of God. That's what I'm offering. A huge relationship with Christ. That's what I'm offering. I'm offering God to every brother and every sister. That's what I'm peddling. I'm peddling a relationship with Christ, who will help you know your value . . . a relationship with Christ, who will help you develop your resource strategy. I'm offering Christ.

I'm offering an intimate and a personal relationship with Christ. And if I were you, before I got in the bed with somebody, I would check with Christ. If I were you, before I decided to commit my resources through sexual access, I would check with Christ. If I were you, I would walk and talk with him.

Study Questions

1. Who is Baby Daddy? Have you met him? Can you describe him?
2. Dr. Thomas says that men need a resource strategy. In pursuit of such a strategy, Jacob stole his brother's blessing to obtain the inheritance for himself. The author describes a number of deceptive means like Jacob's that men use to gain resources. How can we design courses

for boys that will help them avoid negative methods and instead develop good and effective resource strategies for life? The course could include close study and application of the points raised here:

- an income-producing strategy
- a complementing partner
- a support strategy
- a relationship with God

3. Do you believe Dr. Thomas's statement is true pertaining to women wanting men who have resources? Why or why not? Discuss the implications of this statement.

4. Do you believe Dr. Thomas's statement is true pertaining to men valuing sexual access to women? Why or why not? Discuss the implications of this statement.

5. Do you believe that women have the upper hand in dating and more mating opportunities because of their sexuality? Why or why not? Discuss the implications of this statement.

6. Why is it important for men to strengthen their supporting friendships with other men? How can strong relationships between males improve relationships between males and females?

Prayer Thought: O God, may men come to know you and have the faith that you have given to each one something that he may use to develop and achieve a successful resource strategy.

Chapter Ten

And Leah Was Lovely, Too

Genesis 29:16-17, NIV

Now Laban had two daughters; the name of the older was Leah,
and the name of the younger was Rachel. Leah had weak eyes,
but Rachel was lovely in form, and beautiful.

The truth was that Leah was not as physically attractive as Rachel.
The truth was that Leah had a defect in her physical presence. The
Bible says she had weak eyes. Maybe one eye or both eyes drooped or
looked like what we would call a lazy eye, but whatever it was, it ren-
dered her physically unattractive to men. When I searched the commen-
taries to find out more about her defect, nothing turned up. No scholar
would address Leah's physical condition. No one made any comment
about Leah's physical condition. I wonder if it is because looks are so important to us that we are afraid to address Leah's physical condition.

So what is there for Leah? What is there for you when you're disfigured? What is there for you when you are not considered attractive?
What is there for you when you have a sister like Rachel, who the Bible
says was lovely in form and pleasing to the eye? Rachel had a great body
and a delightful face, and therefore she was very popular with men.
What is there for you when you're at the party and nobody will come
over and ask you to dance? What is there for you when you're not the
right size? You're not the right height? Your hair is not the right texture?

Your skin is not the right color? What is there for you when you can't get a date? What is there for you when you learn the tone and the texture of rejection because of your physical features?

I believe that there are some Leahs reading this chapter, both males and females who do not think themselves to be attractive. They do not think that other men and women are paying the right kind of attention to them. I believe there are some sisters who believe themselves to be disfigured in their looks: their breast size ain't the right size; their behind size ain't the right size; their legs ain't the right size. They put this on, and it bulges out over here. They put that on, and it bulges out over there, and nobody will pay attention to them. There are some young brothers who believe that the thugs are getting all the women. These young brothers are trying to do right, trying to serve right and to be right, trying to treat women with respect. These brothers aren't into thug life but can't get the time of day from the sisters. I believe there is something for you. I believe that Leah was lovely, too.

We have been considering a different and somewhat revolutionary way of thinking about male and female relationships—as a business deal instead of as love. In a good business deal, one gives a product or a service in exchange for a product or a service of at least equal value. These essays have suggested that a woman in a relationship ought to obtain a fair value business deal for access to one of her most important assets: her sexuality and her reproductive future. We call this a woman's reproductive strategy.

We have said a man ought to seek fair value for one of his most important assets: the ability to generate resources. We call this a man's resource strategy. These essays have suggested that one of the critical elements of a good relationship is the match between an admirable reproductive strategy and a worthy resource strategy. When such a match occurs, both people in the relationship are getting fair value. And love is easy when both people are getting fair value. Love might be the feeling of getting fair value.

From the perspective of the business deal, a man's wealth and status make the man more attractive to women. Women don't like to admit this. Women would prefer to talk about love, but when mature women tell the truth, they indicate that resources tend to make a man attractive to women regardless of his physical features. You see this every day: an otherwise not-too-attractive star athlete, for example, looks good to many women. He looks like a million dollars to women because, in fact, he does have a million dollars. Physical attractiveness is not as important to women as it is to men. Resources are very important to women.

For many men, a woman's physical attractiveness is what is most desired in the business deal. Many men place a tremendous value on women who are like Rachel, lovely of form and pleasing to look at, and they will give up a whole lot in terms of resources or anything else for an unusually attractive woman. As Matt Ridley says, "Beauty is the trinity of youth, figure, and face,"[1] and men are absolute fools for youth, figure, and face. Men don't like to tell the truth about this, just as women don't like to admit that they are attracted to men's resources, but the truth is that a lot of the men are looking for looks. From the perspective of the business deal, many brothers will take looks and worry about everything else later.

When we deal at the basic level of resources and attractiveness, there's a catch on both sides. A woman's number of mating opportunities is very likely to decline with age, the drop becoming more marked after about forty-five years of age. After physical attractiveness declines, so does the marketability. In effect, this means that women have to be very, very careful because prime time for a woman with one of her most valuable resources—her physical appeal—occurs in her youth when she has the least maturity to be able to handle that very resource. By the time many women figure out what they have and how to deal with it from a mature business perspective, they are already in a complex situation. When men get older, they become distinguished. When women become older, they become . . . older. So women have to be careful because they are cutting lifelong deals for one of their most valuable assets in their youth when they have the least maturity to fully understand the value of those assets.

Most men start with few mating opportunities and low status because they don't have resources. And with few resources, they should not have many sexual opportunities. But men do have sexual opportunities because many women do not know their own value, so they give themselves up to men who have virtually nothing to give back to them. What does a seventeen-year-old male have to give somebody in terms of resources? If the girl has a baby, she has to have it on her parents' or public insurance. Another reason men have sexual opportunities without resources is that men are sometimes able to convey a sense of confidence in their future success. If this confidence is fulfilled, men's attractiveness to women begins to increase as men's success increases. Consider this: a man who achieves considerable success by age forty-five may have more sexual opportunity than he had at twenty. So when he shows up with a little red sports car, it dawns on him that he's attractive. It dawns on him that he's marketable. We call it the midlife crisis. It's a shock when you're more marketable at forty-something than you were at twenty-something. It's a shock for women to be less marketable at forty-something than they were at twenty-something.

By virtue of the resources, the man's marketability is higher than ever. This leads to a successful older man taking a beautiful, much younger wife, the so-called trophy wife who is an ornament of his status and his power. But the young, beautiful wife is no victim because his resources are a symbol of her status and her position. If she outlives her husband, which she is likely to do, she reaps a good inheritance.

When we take love out of it, these relationship dynamics become apparent. This perspective might seem unfamiliar, but young people understand it well. Lil' Kim and Foxy Brown are clear about the value of their sexuality and the kind of resources that men have to provide to be with them. Lil' Kim and Foxy Brown say they will be a man's sex slave if, in fact, they get paid. They have figured out the great value men place on attractiveness and sexuality and how to negotiate their sexuality to get what they want, or they already have the resources they want and they use men for sex and sex alone, similar to the way they think that men use women.

In some sense Foxy Brown and Lil' Kim are a response to the focus on physical attractiveness in male culture. They are clear. "You can lay me, but you sho'nuff got to pay me." Of course many people critique Lil' Kim and Foxy Brown's presentation and focus on material resources for sex as prostitution, but many accept their message as one of the hard, cold realities of life, and—as young people say—"keeping it real."

In this age of keeping it real, you cannot say to kids anymore, "The Bible says Don't have sex!" They ask, "What authority does the Bible have?" Their question is, "What does Notorious Big have to say? What does Jay Z have to say? What does Lil' Kim have to say?" For a lot of youth, these hip-hop cultural icons are more authoritative than the Bible, so you've got to make another kind of translation.

And the translation that I'm trying to make for young people and older people is, God says that marriage is the only place where sexuality is to be freely exchanged, because God understands that women have a valuable resource and may not be mature enough to handle it. God also understands that brothers might not be ready to commit for the rest of their lives to the mother and the child. God says marriage is a safe place to do a business deal involving sexuality and resources because at least there are some legal guarantees and rights that ensure, as much as possible, mutual commitment and investment. I say to the men—Don't go around having sex with everybody, talking about being a real man. A real man does it God's way. In the safety of the marital covenant a real man provides resources.

So I'm trying to direct a sophisticated argument to young men, older men, young women, and older women about the value of what they have to offer and the fair value they are receiving. God understands fair value. That's why I am belaboring the point, for I believe that out-of-control sexuality in our society is adding a deep mood of despair to our communities. And we are *never* going be a free people until we get control of our sexuality.

Leah was disfigured and not desirable to many men. Her father, Laban, tried to marry her off, but he had to give her away in trickery to Jacob because her value was so low. In a culture where a woman's physical attractiveness and beauty was one of the major bartering chips, Leah was in trouble. How could Leah get a fair deal for herself when she was deficient in one of the areas that men value most? What is there for Leah? I realize that it is possible for Leah to decide that she does not want to barter a business deal with a man and to go on to lead a single and fulfilling life instead, but many women do not choose that option. They want to cut a business deal with a man but are lacking in an area most men value.

Well, what can a woman or a man bring to the bargaining table besides looks and resources? Thank God, there is something more valuable than looks or resources. I thank God that there is the possibility of a connection with God. I believe that the rejection of people can put you into a connection with God. And when you are connected with God, God can develop some things in you that are more valuable than looks or resources. We normally do not pay much attention to God's intangibles that affect negotiations because we are focused on physical beauty and resources. God will develop in you inner beauty that I would like to call character. Character is the sum total of attitudes, core beliefs, and dispositions that make up a person's inner countenance or inner spirit. This inner spirit radiates forth to speak louder than the physical and ultimately transforms the physical. The physical we do not have much choice about other than to be responsible stewards with what we have (e.g., workouts, makeup, haircuts, dieting, eating right, breast exam, prostate exam, etc.). But we have a tremendous responsibility to shape and direct our inner character. Regardless of our physical attributes, we can shape and direct our inner countenance that returns to transform our physical appearance.

What I am suggesting is that if someone is not gifted in the area of physical beauty or resources, that is a challenge in his or her life. A challenge is defined as something that you do not change quickly and that will take tremendous strength or courage to deal with. It is our response to challenge that shapes our character and builds our destiny. Euripides said, "We are molding our character and calling it fate." In other words, we do not take up the challenge; we make excuses, and we blame the outcome on someone or something else like fate. God will help you meet the challenge, and in meeting the challenge God will develop character in you. God will mold your character around three principles that are important to God: integrity, personality, and intelligence.

Integrity

The word *integrity* comes from the Latin word *integer,* or "wholeness." It is a whole number or a thing that is complete in itself. Because we are not whole and complete in ourselves, we look for validation from outside of ourselves. Persons who are whole have the quality of honesty and therefore do not have a gap between what they say and what they do. God will make you whole and complete in yourself. You are less likely to make a bad business deal for yourself when you are whole.

Personality

Personality includes the distinctive or noticeable characteristics that make someone socially appealing, such as wit, humor, laughter, or creativity. God will raise these characteristics in you that will function in your spirit to help create the kind of inner spirit that will make you socially appealing.

Intelligence

Intelligence is having the ability to think, reason, or understand in combination with wide knowledge. This results in being quick of mind, a quality that gives one the ability to vary one's behavior in response to the situations of life. Intelligence is the ability to use one's experience to make the best choices in life. God will develop your intelligence.

And when God develops character in you, you become something different and unique. A light begins to beam out of your spirit that transforms external attractiveness or resources and makes you marketable. What I am suggesting is that when you do it God's way, when you live God's way, when you operate your life in God's way, God fundamentally transforms and changes your character on the inside. A light begins to shine on the inside that transcends that with which you have been blessed on the outside. And that is why I can say that Leah was lovely, too. I believe that God transformed Leah's character.

I know what I'm talking about because God transformed my character. When I was in college, there weren't a whole lot of women running after me, trying to make themselves available. I slept alone. I didn't spend the night with anybody. I didn't have many resources. I was in college on a wing and a prayer. I was working in a Chinese restaurant, mopping floors at night. I couldn't buy many of the latest fashions because my parents didn't have the money to give to me. The money that I made in the Chinese restaurant went toward my room and board as my parents and I worked together to pay my college costs. So I didn't have Jordan gym shoes. I didn't have all of that stuff. I had the same old clothes that I had always had because we were scuffling to pay for my education.

My mama used to send me ten dollars a week, and it came on Thursday. I used to long for Thursday. Thank God for Thursday. Now, who are you going to take out for the weekend on ten dollars a week? Where are you going for ten dollars a week? So from a resource perspective, I wasn't very attractive.

Then I was academically in over my head because, as an inner-city kid, I had not been exposed to the same information that a lot of the other students had been exposed to in their suburban high schools. The University of Illinois in Champaign had an admissions requirement of 28 on the ACT, which I didn't have. I had scored 20, but I had worked for a legislator in Springfield who gave me a scholarship that got me into the school. When I arrived on campus, however, and found myself competing with students who had studied in high school things that I was seeing for the first time, I realized that I didn't have a lot of time to clown and mess around. What I had time to do was get to the library.

So I went from the basketball court, to the library, to the church. I remember asking somebody for a date, and her laughing when I asked her. Nothing was happening. Nothing was going on, but I had a relationship with God, and I decided that I was going to try to do it God's way. I decided that I was going to respect women, and when I ever got one, that I was going to treat her right. I was going to act right. I was going to do right. I wasn't going to use and manipulate anybody. My intentions were going to be pure if I ever got anybody. And God began to develop character in me. God began to develop personal inner strength in me, and all of a sudden, I found myself graduating, and I found out that I was attractive to somebody. We went out and got married. Our marriage started out small and insignificant in a little, itty-bitty, rented apartment. We started out with a '69 AMC that her daddy gave to us. The car kept breaking down, so the only way we could continue to drive it was to go over to her father's every Saturday and let him fix it again because we didn't have money to fix it.

My point is that you can watch these videos that portray boys with lots of resources—gold, ships, and planes. But that isn't real for most people. Most men have to start at the bottom with a minimum-wage job. We have to start at the bottom and work our way up. We have to rent a little, itty-bitty apartment and sacrifice and save. My wife and I bought a little insurance policy for ten thousand dollars on each of us when we were married so if one of us died, the other one would have what we thought was big money.

I want you to know that when you stay with God, God builds something. And so my wife and I have been working and building, sacrificing and scuffling, and now we have gotten to a point where we have just a little, and all of a sudden the women come out of the woodwork. But I ask the question, "Where were *y'all* when I was in the library?" I'm clear about this thing. I know who was with me when I had nothing but the promise and hope of the resources. I know who was with me before I was Dr. Thomas. I know who was with me before I had a book. I know who was with me before I had degrees. I know who was with me before I had a lot of members. I know who was with me before I had preaching engagements. I know who was with me when I was a wimp in the library. And I *ain't* confused. God was with me and working for me through the people who supported me like my parents, and especially my wife. God will send somebody to aid and assist you. God will not leave you out there alone. God does not care much about looks and resources; God will transform your character.

I stand before you with a transformed character. I stand before you, and I think that I am lovely, too. I stand before you with intelligence, personality, and integrity because of a God who loves me, and cares for me, and provides for me, and keeps me. You can be lovely, too.

And Leah was lovely, too. I know there are some people in the Bible who were not handsome, attractive, or lovely, but they transformed the world by their inner spirit. It is said of the apostle Paul that he was short and unimpressive, but Paul was a giant before God and the world. Paul wrote two-thirds of the New Testament. John the Baptist was not attractive. The Bible says he went around wearing camel's hair and eating wild locusts and honey, but God chose John the Baptist to prepare the way for the Savior of the world. And then there was the one of whom the text says, "he hath no form nor comeliness; and when we shall see him, there is no beauty that we should desire him. He is despised and rejected of men; a man of sorrows, and acquainted with grief: and we hid as it were our faces from him; he was despised, and we esteemed him not. Surely he hath borne our griefs, and carried our sorrows. . . . But he was wounded for our transgressions, he was bruised for our iniquities . . . and with his stripes we are healed" (Isaiah 53:2-5, KJV).

The suffering servant was lovely, too. John the Baptist was lovely, too. The apostle Paul was lovely, too. And Leah was lovely, too.

---

[1] Matt Ridley. *The Red Queen: Sex and the Evolution of Human Nature* (New York: Penguin, 1993).

Study Questions

1. What importance do you attach to physical attractiveness? For a male? For a female?
2. Why does society seem to attach so much importance to physical attractiveness?
3. What advantages do physically attractive people enjoy (not only in this society, but everywhere and throughout history)?
4. Are physically unattractive people discriminated against? How?
5. Why do the qualities of integrity, personality, and intelligence transcend physical attractiveness? Discuss each one separately.
6. What made Leah and the other biblical persons mentioned at the end of this chapter lovely, too?

Prayer Thought: Physical attractiveness is never enough. May the beautiful and the not so beautiful both possess inner qualities that, unlike beauty, do not fade with the passing of time.

Chapter Eleven

An Enabling Escape

Genesis 29-30

I wonder if the role of Leah in this text is similar to the role of many women today. Leah was doomed to a fate and trapped in a cycle that still seems much too prevalent. We know from previous essays that Jacob loved Rachel over Leah. We know that Leah did not have the physical graces and the outward attractiveness of Rachel. We know that the only way Leah got married was that her father tricked Jacob into the marriage, substituting her for her sister, Rachel, on the wedding night. We know that Jacob loved Rachel and tolerated Leah. Leah was trapped in a relationship, trying to get a man to love her who obviously had eyes for another woman. The best she could do was to have babies for him and hope that he would love her because she bore him many sons.

So, after the birth of the first baby, Leah cries the sorrowful refrain, "Maybe he will love me now." After the second son she laments, "Maybe he will become attached to me now." After another son she states, "Maybe he will care for me. Maybe he will listen to me. Maybe, maybe, maybe." It's a sorrowful refrain that comes down through the pages of these twenty-ninth and thirtieth chapters of Genesis. And we find Leah is trapped in a kind of hell on earth.

I have often wondered if damnation is the fate of some women. I have wondered if hell on earth is the position of trying to get somebody to love you; changing your personality, trying to get somebody to love you; dressing in other than what you like, trying to get somebody to love you; changing the way you talk, trying to get somebody to love you; giving up sex, trying to get somebody to love you; having his baby, trying to get somebody to love you. I wonder if hell on earth is trying to get somebody to do something that he does not want to do, especially to love you. Leah was in hell right here on earth, trying to get Jacob to love her.

In all fairness to Leah, we must remember that women in her day did not have many options. It was the function of women to have babies and to win the love of their husbands. Women were considered property whose chief occupation was to bear children and serve men. Not many people were interested in the hopes and dreams of women. Not many people were interested in whether a woman had a self. Women were property who were to serve at the whim of men. A woman's self was tied to a man's. A woman who was not able to bear children was in a very, very bad position because a woman's value was not in and of herself but as an appendage to a man.

I wonder if it is still true, despite our modern times, despite career options, and despite women's liberation, that many women are doing the same thing Leah did: trying to get some man to love them. I'm not just talking about poor women, either, for I know some educated women, I know some degree-laden women, I know some women who make nice money, I know some affluent women who are doing the same thing that Leah is doing in this text: trying to get some man to love them. All these women are adjusting themselves, trying to get some man to care about them. They're having sex, trying to get somebody to commit to them. They're having babies, trying to get somebody to pay attention and to love them. You sentence yourself to hell on earth, trying to get somebody to love you.

What I have tried to propose in these essays, however, is not just an escape from hell. What I have tried to propose is not just a way to get out of a bad situation, but what I have been proposing is an enabling escape.

Not just escape from a life that is in constant pursuit of the love of men, but an escape from a life that lacks identity and self to an enabling life with a God-given destiny and a God-given call. A life with the authority to manage and maximize one's own present and future according to one's own wants, needs, and desires—an enabling life. A life that has power, not necessarily over people, but the greatest power on earth, which is the authority to be whom God has made one to be. To be one's self. To live for one's self. To listen for one's self. To take a vacation for one's self. To go to school for one's self. To laugh for one's self. To cry for one's self. To be concerned about one's self. To think about one's self. Not just to escape a dependent love cycle, but also to be one's self—an enabling escape. Not just learning how to live without the love of a man but learning how to live for one's self—an enabling escape.

To help bring clarity to what I mean by an enabling escape, I must talk about what I believe it is necessary for women to escape from. I believe that we all seek escapes because the most difficult thing in the world is to truly face life for what life is. A whole lot of us are in denial about the realities of life because they are so painful, so we construct realities of denial to avoid both the truth and the incessant pain that goes with the truth.

Life is fragile, uncertain, and unsure, and we don't like to face this. In fact, nothing in this life is guaranteed. You can be well today and get sick tomorrow. You can have a good job today and be unemployed tomorrow. You can live in a nice home today and find yourself on the street tomorrow. Life is uncertain. Some of us *will* get cancer. Some of us *will* be downsized. Some of us *will* get sick. Our loved ones *will* walk out on us. People *will* betray us. So we construct realities of denial in order to cope with life's uncertainties. A lot of us relate to God and church this way, wanting God and the pastor to guarantee that we will not have to face fragility and uncertainty. But God does not function as a genie in a bottle. *What God wants to do is build in us spiritual reserves that allow us to have victory in the midst of fragility, uncertainty, and the things that are unsure in life.* God is not going to take away all of our suffering. God is not going to take away all of our tragedy. God gives strength in the midst of suffering. I don't care how many prayer cloths we get, some of us are going to have cancer. I don't care how many times we tithe, some of our children are going to come up on drugs. Suffering is a part of the matrix of life. It takes most of us many years to accept this fact of suffering as one of the basic realities of life.

But women have to deal with another painful reality—the reality of being second-class citizens in this world. Almost every woman reaches a point where she discovers that it's a man's world. There are many examples to demonstrate this truth, but let's consider health issues. First, compared with men, women in disproportionately large numbers fill the doctors' offices, clinics, psychiatrists' offices, therapists' offices, and pastors' offices seeking professional care. I am willing to grant that many men deny their health problems and do not come in for professional help as easily and regularly as women do, but I believe women's visits are directly related to their stress from being second-class citizens. And if that is not enough, though women seek medical care in far greater numbers than men do and pay more into the health care system, far less money is spent on medical research for women's illnesses than for men's illnesses.

Nevertheless, the knowledge of this world's discriminatory way does not let women off the hook, just as being black with higher incidences of stress-related diseases than the majority population doesn't allow us to place the blame for all of our problems on white people. Such blaming serves only as an excuse. Instead, women and others who experience discrimination must respond by determining to shape their character and destiny. Second-class citizenship is a challenge. As I have said before, a challenge is something that you do not change quickly or easily. How we respond to challenge shapes our character and our destiny. So don't tell me that they won't let you in. Don't tell me that it's a man's world out there and you can't be what you want to be and do what you want to do because it's a man's world. No. Shape your character. Don't make excuses. Shape your destiny.

Of course, shaping one's character and destiny is a process that takes time. So typically, to deal with the pain, women construct and become fixated on a reality that they call love and romance. The constructed reality of love and romance is in the culture and the thinking of most girls and most women. One facet of this constructed reality is the belief that women give up any and everything for love. Therefore, love and the search for love are the prime and motivating factors in a woman's life, and a woman should sacrifice everything for love. A woman confesses, "I'm being physically abused, but I love him." I ask, "What does love have to do it?" She complains, "No rent is being paid, no lights, gas, or electricity are on, but I love him." I ask, "What does love have to do with that?" I am not against love, but we must open our understanding of love to include a fair business deal. There is nothing wrong with love and romance, but we must teach that love is not love if there is not the responsible sharing of resources. Or, as some of my friends say, "There is definitely no romance without finance!"

We have learned as men and women, but primarily women, to fuse romance, love, sex, and reproduction. Girls receive countless cues, countless experiences, and countless stories to fuse romance, love, sex, and reproduction. The romance literature is full of this fusion—Beauty and the Beast, Cinderella, and a thousand other stories. Teenage girls say they love romance novels with stories of love and dating because the stories allow them to escape. The place that they escape to is the land of romance: a place where girls wait for love and receive it; a place where boys love the girls before and after sex; a place where kids are products of a happy relationship and where the family lives happily ever after; a place where femininity tames, or at least relieves, the wild beast that is in men. Men are like beasts, but women have such beauty and love that it tames or relieves the savage beast in men.

Not only do romance novels portray this cultural ethos, but much of everyday television and television commercials are based on this notion, too. While I was working on this manuscript, I took a break and watched a tennis match on television. A beer commercial was on that showed a room full of brothers, sitting around watching the game, all having a good time. Then someone knocked on the door, and one of the brothers opened it, and a "babe" walked in dressed in a short, black dress. She was like the biblical Rachel, lovely of form and pleasing to the eye. She said, "I'm your new neighbor, and I've got some boxes that I need help with." The brothers, who were holding cans of beer, were in that moment caught up in the power of the magnificent feminine mystique, and their whole world stopped. She perused her captive audience and saw that one of these brothers had a Colt 45 in his hand, and because he had what to her was the right beer, she said, "I'll take you."

The commercial exploited in the extreme the deeply ingrained cultural and somewhat factual belief that erotic femininity will make men grovel with desire. The commercial demonstrated that female sexuality can rock the world of most men. This notion taken to the extreme entices some women to trade and forego their equality with men for the illusion of female sexual power. Some people critique Foxy Brown and Lil' Kim on the basis that they entice women to give up any vision of equality for the illusion of female sexual power. Men are beasts, but women have such beauty and love that it tames the savage beast. Typically, this type of romance was the acknowledged female adventure. Men went off to war, to the hunt, or to work. Women stayed behind and prepared themselves for the erotic love and passion that would occur when their warriors, hunters, and breadwinners returned home.

The uncritical adoption of romantic thinking leads women to being victimized because naïve romantic thinking establishes unrealistic expectations that are rarely fulfilled in this life. Many women and girls wait for love and don't get it. For some it starts as love but ends up as something else. Some boys do not love the girls after sex. And many times, after women tame or relieve the beast, the beast shows up again. Many children are not the products of a happy relationship. A critical factor in the victimization of women is the extent to which women fuse romance, love, sex, and reproduction, and thereby do not give enough importance to the business side of relationships and life. Sharon

Thompson says this, "Once in love or set on getting love, women close their eyes to sexual and psychological danger."[1] The man says, "Trust me, babe. I don't have a condom, but trust me. Trust me." Her response should be "I don't know where you've been." They ought to have a marriage license before they do anything, anyway. But he says, "Trust me." There are diseases that can take her life, and because she fuses romance, love, sex, and reproduction, she is blinded and will allow somebody not even to put a condom on? Once in love or set on acquiring love, many women close their eyes to sexual and psychological danger.

Thompson says that love is a hard argument for women and girls to reject. She adds, "even when [it is] mixed with violence or condescension or paternalistic control."[2]

I understand a woman's need for affection, but *the love that would be the most helpful for women would be a love that understands not only her need for affection but also her need for a separate identity, continued growth, recognition, and equality.* That's what love is. That's what I'm talking about when I keep asking, "What does love have to do with it?" When a man at least attempts to recognize your separate identity and supports continued growth, when a man treats you with equality and not as though you were less than he is, that, in my opinion, is love. I'm saying there is a difference between love and blind neediness. What many videos and love songs often describe is blind neediness and desperation. When blind neediness and desperation are the generating forces of love, an accident is about to occur, and damage is in the psychological neighborhood. The true force of love is affection, recognition, and equality. The true force of love permits and encourages separate identities and continued growth.

The sad odds are that many women will get locked in just like Leah did. The odds are that many women will get caught in fusing love, romance, sex, and reproduction. The odds are that women will spend too much time in their lives trying to get some man to love them. The odds are that many women won't escape. And so, I'm not just shooting for you to escape; I'm saying that with God you can have an enabling escape. Not only can you escape the trap that has been set, but also you can discover identity and self, equality, recognition, and affection. And if you don't get it from somebody outside of yourself, you can discover it for yourself, within yourself. I'm going to put some practical things on your plate that will assist your enabling escape.

Don't Fuse Romance, Love, Sex, and Reproduction

You cannot fuse romance, love, sex, and reproduction. There are four stages in relationships: romance, love, sex, and reproduction. Romance is the first stage. The fact that you're in the stage of romance does not mean that you are in the stage of love. Love is a separate and a distinct stage, and the fact that you're in love does not mean that you move to the sexual stage. That's a different stage. And reproduction is another stage after the sexual stage.

First there is romance. After romance, there's a transition to love. Once love is established, there's a marriage license and a transition to sex. After a time of sex in the context of marriage, the couples check their reproductive and resource strategies and decide on reproduction. A woman who fuses these four things, making them the center of her life, is in hell because the central meaning of one's life cannot be found in the fusion of romance, love, sex, and reproduction. Kisses are not contracts, and there is a difference between playing house and making a home. The central meaning of one's life is to be found only in God.

Stop Playing the Victim

Stop playing the victim and take responsibility for your life. You can refuse melodrama. Melodrama is the extreme glorification of a relationship with a man. Melodrama paints all women as innocent and all men as dogs. And so women parlay their innocence and naïveté into great pain that is called melodrama. When a woman is pretending to be naïve and is playing innocent, and she encounters a foolish man and gets hurt, then she wants to take out a razor and slit her wrists because the man didn't call after they had sex. But I'm saying, check yourself out, because the reason you had sex is that you fused romance, love, and sex all together in one. I'm saying it ain't that serious except that you make it that serious, because what you're doing is using love and romance to keep from dealing with the realities of life—that life is fragile and that you're a second-class citizen. So you construct a reality of love and romance and look for somebody to drop it on. And when you uncritically drop it on someone, he is likely to abuse your love and you.

You can tell that a woman is being melodramatic when she generalizes her disappointment with one man to all men. "All men are dogs," she says. No, all men are not dogs. There are a lot of good men. It may be that the last five she was with were dogs, but then she has to ask some questions about her interviewing and selection processes. But we don't want to ask tough questions. We want to be victims. We want to be melodramatic. But stop playing the victim and take responsibility for your life, and you will discover that some men don't deserve even to get an interview.

Balance Love with Other Concerns

Balance the desire for love with an array of other concerns in relationships. Don't give up all of your dreams for love. The most visible, tangible evidence of this is somebody who can hang around with the girlfriends. They're tight as long as she doesn't have a man. But when a man enters her life, she drops all of her friends, and her sole interest is the man who is wonderful, beautiful, and lovely. I am suggesting that you don't give up all of your friends because you find somebody. Keep your friends. Balance. Keep your hopes and dreams. Don't give up all your hopes and dreams to work on someone else's hopes and dreams. Don't uncritically put a man through medical or law school without some agreements relative to your hopes and dreams. What about your hopes, and what about your dreams? Sometimes both of you can't go to school at the same time, but there ought to be a plan for balance.

Don't Give Yourself Away

Never give yourself into anybody else's keeping. Don't give your whole heart to anybody else. There's only one who can contain your whole heart, and that's God. Don't give anybody your whole heart. Don't give anybody your whole self. He will not know what to do with it. When you give yourself over to somebody, he will fumble you because he doesn't know what to do with you. He hardly knows what to do with himself, let alone you. The love that is sometimes practiced in this world is ephemeral. It can be quick. It can be fleeting. It can be here today and gone tomorrow. They've gone on a cruise together today, hugged up at the captain's table, but she's cutting him out of the picture tomorrow. Don't give yourself over to anybody but God.

Don't Let Love Cause You to Harm Yourself

No matter how much in love you are or how much love you need, refuse to accept love as a reason to endanger yourself. Why are you going to endanger yourself for love? Why are you going to lie down with some brother and endanger yourself psychologically? No marriage license. No condom. Just sex. He's married, but you're so hungry for love. Endangerment. Is that love? To put yourself at risk? Is that love? Refuse to accept love as a reason to endanger yourself or foreclose your future. Protect yourself. If anybody has a problem with your protecting yourself, *that ain't love*. Don't endanger yourself. Don't foreclose your future. That's not love. That's blind neediness. That's desperation masquerading as love, because where there is love, there is acceptance, and recognition, and equality, and separate identities, and a commitment to your continued growth. Oh, that's love!

I want to close with prayer because some of these situations are so very, very painful. There are places in my own life where I have violated some of the five things that I warn you against. I've been there, and I've certainly seen people there who are important to me. I believe there are some secrets that sisters dare not tell. I believe some sisters are looking good and are sharp, but they are like Leah. I'm saying that God will give you an enabling escape, but God will give it to you if you deal with some of the things that we have talked about. So you reread this chapter until the dialogue is no longer between you and me but between you and God because you've got to talk to God about where you are. You've got to talk to God about what you need to do. You talk to God, and God will talk to you, and the conversation will be about you and God. I am going to pray that right now.

> **Prayer:** Dear God, I thank you for those who have taken the time to read this essay. I thank you for their willingness to allow these words to confront their lives. I ask that you strengthen and encourage them. I know that lives are at stake and children are at stake. I know that marriages and families are at stake, and I would like for you to move to center stage and take control. Help someone to see how you are speaking to him or her in this essay. Help someone to see what you would have him or her to do. Help someone to escape. Give that one an enabling escape. I thank you because only you can do it. You are the God who allowed Jesus an enabling escape from Calvary. Do the same in someone's life. Amen.

---

[1] Sharon Thompson. *Going All The Way: Teenage Girls' Tales of Sex, Romance, and Pregnancy* (New York: Hill and Wang, 1995), 240.

[2] Ibid.

Study Questions

1. Dr. Thomas wonders out loud in this essay if the damnation caused by trying to make someone love you is the unhappy fate of some women. Why is it futile to try to get someone to love you?

2. An enabling escape is a positive way to deal with the painful realities of life. Discuss the fact that life is painful and that people do seek means of escaping life's pain. What are some of the most common escapes that people use? Have you considered that many love relationships are entered into for the purpose of escaping life's pain?

3. How can persons avoid using relationships to escape pain?

4. Should shaping one's character and destiny take precedence over establishing a love relationship? Why? Does being involved in a love relationship help or hinder the shaping of one's character and destiny? How?

5. Dr. Thomas quotes an author in this chapter who says that love is understanding a woman's need for affection as well as her need for a separate identity, continued growth, recognition, and equality. Is this an acceptable definition of the love of a male for a female? Explain why or why not. Could the same definition apply to the love of a female for a male? Explain.

6. Illustrate how someone may accomplish an enabling escape from life's pain by using the following principles, giving an example for each one:
   • Don't fuse romance, love, sex, and reproduction
   • Stop playing the victim
   • Balance love with other concerns
   • Don't give yourself away
   • Don't let love cause you to harm yourself

Prayer Thought: O God, thank you for an enabling escape from the kind of suffering that diminishes our human dignity.

Chapter Twelve

Sexcapades

Genesis 29-32

Throughout this collection of essays, I have been grappling with love, power, sex, and God in relationships. For a significant part of the series, I have struggled with my belief that women tend to give their power away in hopes of receiving romance and love from men. I have suggested that it is not that women are powerless; women have tremendous power, but many women give away their power, trying to get love and romance. Women fuse romance, love, sex, and reproduction and end up in physically and psychologically dangerous, high-risk situations. Thus, my attempt has been to challenge women to stop blaming men for their conditions and look at the ways and means by which they who are so powerful readily and easily give up their power. It is not that women are powerless; it's that women have agreed to give up their power, trying to get love and romance.

My challenge to women is to stop blaming things on men. Stop talking about the men that ran you down. Stop talking about bad fathers. Stop talking about all of that, and talk more about the ways and means by which women so readily and so easily give up their God-given power and authority in relationships. Even though I have not blamed men for the condition of women, some of the brothers are worrying that the entire experience and perspective of men will not enter the discussion. Usually there is only one kind of man who comes up in the discussion: the man who is pitiful, the man who is trifling, the man who is pathetic, the man who doesn't show up as father, the man who doesn't stay with the family, the man who drinks, and the man who chases women. What about the brothers who are in there struggling and fighting to do what is right? What about the brothers who exhibit tremendous amounts of strength, energy, and effort, trying to hold a family together, trying to get the bills paid, trying to help raise the kids, trying to be a role model, and trying to develop a resource strategy? As one brother asked me, "What do you do, Pastor Frank, when you're trying to pay the child support, but the mama will in no way cooperate and is using access to the child as a weapon?"

"Pastor Frank, what about when the mother is on drugs and she takes the child support money and snorts it?" asked another.

And another, "Pastor Frank, what about some of these courtrooms that are so unfamiliar with a man trying to do the right thing that you get the hammer dropped on you regardless as to whether or not you are trying to do the right thing?"

These brothers were asking questions and trying to tell me that it is tremendously difficult and painful to try to do the right thing. They were saying that not all brothers are treating women viciously. There are many men who are trying to do the right thing, and not many sermons are written for and not much respect is given to them. I wrote this essay to encourage the brothers who are trying to do the right thing. On behalf of all of the brothers who try, let me say that it hurts. It's not easy. It's a whole lot of work.

I know that we are more familiar discussing the pain of women than we are discussing the pain of men, but men, like women, seek to escape pain in life. The most difficult thing in the world is to face life for what life is. That is my definition of maturity. A mature person is able to face life for what life is. But being unable to face life for what life really is, men, as well as women, construct fantasies to handle life's pain. Just like women, men have to face the reality that they can be healthy today and sick tomorrow.

Men have to face the fact that their loved one might walk away from them. Men have to face the fact that they might have to deal with prostate cancer. Men discover that there are no guarantees and that life is fragile and uncertain and brings a tremendous amount of anxiety. On top of that, black men are living in a culture that is dominated by white males, which brings its own areas of stress and anxiety on top of the basic anxiety of life.

I suggest this not to give anybody an excuse: the white man won't let you do this and the white man won't let you do that. No. I don't want to hear about what the white man won't let you do, for a man should regard anything difficult in life as a challenge. Men's and women's characters are built in response to challenge. And how you respond to challenges shapes your character and your destiny. Don't give me an excuse about a glass ceiling over your head; don't tell me that they've given all the jobs to the black women because they want to hold the black men back. No. Shape your character, and build your destiny. Stand up with your gifts. Go ahead and do the best that you can. Don't you know that God will somehow work everything out all right? Notwithstanding the fact that we refrain from making excuses, black men still must face being black males in a predominantly white-male-dominated world. The ordinary adverse circumstances of life and the lack of power in a white-male-dominated society contribute to the pain that black men experience.

I believe that men use sex to escape these two realities. To deal with the pain and to cope with it, men construct a reality of sexual fantasy. I call it sexcapades. They construct a reality of sex capers, sex fantasy, and outrageous sex encounters. Borrowing from icecapades, I call it sexcapades because an icecapade show is one with swirling colored lights shining on athletes who perform sensational flips and back flips that tantalize the audience. The audience comes for a heightened experience, a fantasy that is almost real. We know we are looking at something make-believe, but for a while we can pretend that it is real. This is what sexcapades are: flipping, and turning, and lights, and a bunch of heightened sexual experiences that are not real, all done to try to deal with the reality of how painful life is. So men construct a reality of outrageous sexual encounter, and one woman won't do, two women won't do, three women won't do. As Magic Johnson suggested, it got up to six.

This constructed false reality of sexcapades is in the culture and thinking of most boys and most men. The fundamental assumption of this reality is, if the sex is good enough, it will take away all of the pain. If I could just have sex with the right one, then it would erase the pain. This leads to an overemphasis by many men on women's looks and body parts. It leads to a fascination with external appearance, and many men almost do anything because of their physical attraction to a woman. Most men receive countless cultural cues and have and hear of innumerable experiences that lead them to fuse sex with a release from pain. That's why I say it's in the cultural thinking of most boys and men because from the time the male child comes out of the womb, he gets messages to fuse sex with a release from pain. Just watch any of these beer commercials and you will see gorgeous, bikini-clad women. The fantasy is ridiculous, but the message is that all beauty and healing, all transformation and love, and all goodness and kindness for men are found in a sexual relationship with a woman. If a man will just get the right woman, it will happen for him.

Men think, "If I could just get with that; if I could just have her, then it would be all right. I'll promise anything. I'll say anything. I'll send anything to get sex." Many men escape to a land of hard bodies and cute faces. They escape to bikini-clad beaches and skin-tight parties, a place where women want sex without commitment; a place where men can get it on with whoever turns them on without hesitance, restriction, or resistance. In other words, women will give men what men want in the way men want it without demanding a marriage license, a resource strategy, or even any communication. So, many men travel to a place of sexual fantasy where pregnancy does not exist, or if it does exist, it is not thought about because it is not a male concern. That's a woman's concern, men think. She ought to know how to take care of herself.

Sexcapades is a sport that boys and men play to demonstrate conquest and power: how many women they can get, how often they can get them, and who can they tell that they got them? Sexcapades is a sport, featuring uncles sitting on porches, watching young boys with girls, grilling the boys: "You gettin' some of that? You bangin' that? Then, go ahead on. You doin' all right, son," as if male value is found in our sexuality.

The problem with the land of sexcapades is that it is based on a tremendous lie: that sex can deal with the complexity of one's pain. It's called pornography. Pornography is the belief that sex can handle the pain. If I can see the right body, or be with the right body, in the right shape, in the right position, then life won't hurt anymore. It's called pornography, and many men are pornographic. We are raised with it in the culture. We are raised with it in the thinking. We have come to believe that sex can overcome the fundamental pain of living in this world.

And you must see that I'm not trying to blame anyone. I am trying to suggest that men and women are in partnership. I believe that women trade sex to get love, and men trade love to get sex. So the pornographic male meets the love-starved female, and they get in relationship. And when the pornographic male runs into the love-starved female, the pornographic male is surprised at how dependent the love-starved female is and how much love and relationship she wants. And the love-starved female is surprised at how addicted to parts and body the pornographic male is, and so the female and the male get together and surprise each other with their level of neediness and desperation.

Brothers in my congregation have acknowledged to me that they were raised in the pornographic culture. Some of them have acknowledged the urge in them to focus on the physical and to see the role of women as toys for the pleasure of men. But they are trying to get rid of that. They are trying to raise a family. They are trying to treat a woman right. They're trying to go to work. They're trying, though not always successful. They fall down and make some mistakes sometimes, but it is in their heart to do the right thing. It is in their heart to be the right thing. Some brothers are turning down the land of sexcapades.

Some brothers are into respecting the women in their lives—

wives, girlfriends, mothers, daughters, sisters, and aunts—as people with separate identities and the need for continued growth. Some brothers are into giving affection, recognition, and equality. These brothers want to be encouraged in their doing of the right thing, and they want their story told.

To tell their story we must locate Jacob, whose name means "trickster." Jacob was quite a trickster. He tricked his brother, Esau, out of his birthright and also out of their father's blessing. When Jacob and his mama tricked Esau out of Esau's blessing, Esau got angry and wanted to kill Jacob. So their mother, Rebekah, told Jacob, "You had better go see Uncle Laban until the heat dies down." When Jacob reached his Uncle Laban's land, he met his cousin, Rachel. Now, Rachel had a great body and a cute face. Rachel was bad, and so the Bible says that Jacob instantly fell in love with Rachel. The Bible says there was a large stone covering a well, and it took many men to move that stone. But when Jacob saw Rachel, he moved the stone by himself.

Jacob wanted Rachel and was willing to agree to Laban's terms that he work for seven years to have her as his wife. The problem was that Rachel had an older sister named Leah who had a disfigured face. She had a weak eye, so Leah was not attractive to brothers because brothers are basically pornographic. Daddy Laban had a hard time finding a mate for daughter Leah, so what Daddy did was concoct a scheme and substitute Leah for Rachel on the wedding night. When Jacob woke up the next morning and found out he had been with Leah, Laban agreed to give him Rachel, too, but demanded that Jacob work another seven years for Rachel. So now Jacob has Rachel and Leah, and there is a problem because, like many people who are in marriages that were forced by circumstances, Leah and Jacob have no real bond of love, and Leah is continually trying to get Jacob to love her. You're in hell when you're trying to get somebody to love you.

As the story continued, Laban and Jacob fell out, so Jacob got word from God that he ought to go home, and as he was thinking about this, he remembered Esau. But it got worse and worse with Laban, so Jacob decided to sneak out during the night with the daughters, the goods, and everything that he had worked so hard for, for twenty years, without telling Uncle Laban. When Uncle Laban got up and found out that Jacob was gone, he caught up with him, and the two argued. They resolved their differences and made a covenant.

Jacob prepared to meet Esau on his way back home. Because he had done Esau so much wrong, he sent a peace offering ahead to his brother. He is now standing at the River Jabok, having sent his wives and eleven sons and one daughter over the river, followed by his possessions, and he is standing all alone.

Your antennae ought to be up, for when somebody sends all of his possessions, all of his titles, all of his degrees, all of his family, all of his money, all of his trophies, all of his worldly interests, all of his clothes, all of his shoes—everything—across the river and hangs out on the other side, I believe that he is getting ready for a radical encounter. The Bible says, "So Jacob was left alone" (Genesis 32:24, NIV). No rescuer. No help. No sex. No money. Jacob was left all alone. No friends. No bank account. No church members. No pastor. No deacons. No ushers. Jacob was left all alone. It was essential for the struggle that was about to ensue that he be all by himself.

The Bible says that while he is left utterly and entirely alone, he is attacked, and before he knows it, he is wrestling with someone or something. Make no mistake about it—the struggle is an attack. It's a sneak attack like the attack of a murderer or a robber. When a murderer or a robber attacks someone, there are specific kinds of conditions: the victim is usually alone, the victim is virtually defenseless, the victim is utterly taken by surprise, it is usually at night, and the attacker must conceal his identity and not reveal his name. All of these conditions were operative for Jacob when the attack came.

This was a robber. This was a murder attempt. This was an ambush. This was an attack. Now I know that this interpretation of the text is very different from what you are used to hearing. You are used to hearing that Jacob was wrestling with an angel, not with a robber. Well, it might be that the angel was a robber. There is some thinking in the Old Testament that Satan was an angel, and if you look carefully at the development of the theology of evil, biblical scholars say that Satan once worked for God. It is also thought that Satan and God once had a pretty good relationship. It is said that it was the role of Satan to go to and fro on earth to see what was going on. Satan then made his report to God. This thinking is reflected in the Book of Job, where we see Satan going to and fro on earth, gathering information for his report.

Across time, the role of Satan goes from reporting to entrapping. In this text, the role of Satan moves from building up saints to entrapment, and from entrapment to accusation. By the time of the New Testament, Satan has become the accuser of the saints, as well as the one who entraps. When we fall into the trap, then Satan tells God, "See. They don't amount to much. They're mine. See. They're not very good Christians. They're mine." This is the role of Satan. It is possible in this text that Jacob was wrestling with a messenger of Satan, who is connected to God.

I know that this is radical theology, but I believe that God allows Satan to tempt and test us. I believe that the temptations and the tests are meant to strengthen our character and our courage. I believe that ultimately Satan serves the purposes of God. I believe that Satan attempts to entrap and accuse us but in the test we become stronger and better Christians. I believe that Jacob is wrestling with what might be a robber or murderer sent to test Jacob.

I believe that many men experience a test similar to Jacob's. Many men are tested in the area of sexuality. I believe that sexcapades slip up on some men. The family is gone away, and the possessions are gone away, and all of a sudden out of nowhere, you're attacked. You can be sitting in church, trying to worship and praise God, and you look around, and all of a sudden, you are attacked with sexual fantasy. You can be at a basketball game, trying to pay attention, and all of a sudden, you find yourself waffling with a certain kind of fling based upon some cheerleader that you see. It comes out of nowhere. I don't care how saved and how sanctified and how filled you are with the Holy Ghost. Every now and then, you find yourself in a wrestling match. You find yourself distracted. *You find yourself paying attention to what you ain't got no business paying attention to.* Before you know it, you're in a wrestling match. Got your wedding ring on, but you're in a wrestling match. Committed with a fiancée, but already you find yourself in a wrestling match. Have five kids, been married thirty-five years, and you're in a wrestling match. *Sexual fantasy is a powerful force and a difficult temptation for many men.*

But notice that Jacob is equal to the task. The fact that he wrestled all night suggests persistence, determination, and an unwillingness to give up. He struggled and did not quit. Sexcapades is a prolonged struggle for many men. And there are many men out there who are fighting the good fight. They are just like Jacob, equal to the task and struggling with persistence and determination. Not every brother is sleeping around. Not every brother is partaking of pornographic fantasy. Many brothers are faithful and devoted and keep the commitment to one woman. Many brothers struggle to do the right thing. Many brothers are wrestling like Jacob. And as Jacob was successful, many brothers are successful, too.

I think that what a lot of the brothers are trying to say to me and what they want me to say as I preach is that there are some real temptations out there, but they're equal to the task. I think the brothers want to say, "It's a real temptation to get a younger woman; it's a real temptation to get mad and leave; it's a real temptation, but some brothers are equal to the task. Some of the brothers are wrestling with this thing, wrestling for their relationship, wrestling for their marriage, wrestling for their family, wrestling to be fathers, even though they and the mama are split up. They're still wrestling, trying to maintain their relationship with the children. Still wrestling with this thing. They are equal to the task.

Some of the women are like Rachel, lovely of form and pleasing to the eye, and are available and willing to be in a compromising relationship. But it's not what a brother sees that gets him into trouble; it's what he does with what he sees. It is the level of fantasy that he attaches to what he sees. The level of fantasy you attach to what you see has to do with the level of pain in your life. What you do with what you see has to do with the level of pain in your life. The woman that you see is a regular flawed human being, but men add fantasy in an attempt to handle the pain in their lives. We make the woman into more than she really is for our own purposes. And it is interesting to me that many men, after they have the one they are fantasizing about, throw the woman away in disappointment, never realizing, of course, that the need was so great in them that no woman could have satisfied the need.

Jacob was equal to the task. Maybe Jacob dealt with the pain in his life. When the robber saw that Jacob was equal to the task, the Bible says, he touched the socket of Jacob's hip to further limit Jacob's ability to wrestle. The Bible says, even hurt and wounded, Jacob kept wrestling. Jacob wrestled with the man to the extent that the man asked to be released. The man said, "Let me go, for the day breaks." Jacob responded, "I will not let you go until you bless me." Jacob believed this messenger was sent to test him and now that he had passed the test, the man had to bless him. God allows Satan to tempt and to test you, but when you have wrestled with the test, Satan has to bless you. Satan will ask you to allow him to leave, and you will say, "You cannot leave until you bless me." The man turns to Jacob and says, "And your name will no longer be called Jacob, but Israel because you have struggled with God and with men and prevailed." And the man blessed Israel there.

There are some men who have received new names. They, like Jacob, were called *trickster*, but now they are called *Israel*. Some were once called *pimp*, but now they are called *preacher*. Some were once called *whoremonger*, but now they are called a *husband of one wife*. Some were once called *dogs*, but now they are called *daddy in the home*. Some were once called *pornographers*, but now they are called *people of purity*. Some were called *players*, but now they are called *pau-pau*. I thank God for new names. I thank God for all the brothers who have new names and who are doing the right thing.

Study Questions

1. According to Dr. Thomas, men construct sexual fantasies to help them deal with the pain of living. Mentally and morally destructive, these fantasies lead to "sexcapades"—outrageous sexual encounters—that men believe will alleviate their pain. Discuss this concept.

2. Dr. Thomas says that sexcapades are nothing more than pornography and thus unable to help men handle life's pain. Why is pornography so prevalent in our society? Should its distribution be protected by First Amendment rights of free speech? Or should the government control or work to eliminate the distribution of pornography?

3. How helpful would it be to acknowledge pornographic thinking as part of the cultural conditioning of most males? How might we begin to change this conditioned thinking?

4. The story of Jacob, Leah, and Rachel, which has run throughout this book, appears in this last chapter as Jacob wrestles with his demon and wins. This is a fitting metaphor for what many men wrestle with in the area of sexual temptation. How can the church encourage males to fight against the prevailing pornographic culture and win for themselves, their families, their communities, and their God?

5. The underlying theme in this book has been that neither males nor females are helpless victims of misguided cultural norms that affect relationships. What lessons in this book have made an impact on your life and thinking? In what ways have you changed the ways in which you look at yourself and others with respect to love and relationships? Can you answer the question "What's love got to do with it?"

Prayer Thought: O God, deliver males from the pursuit of sexcapades as a means of escaping their pain. May they wrestle with their demons and be victorious in you.

Look for an accompanying workbook and related products by the author.

Contact Dr. Frank Thomas at www.Hope4life.net

Hope For Life International, Inc. is a 501 (c)(3) non-profit organization facilitating the global preaching, teaching, writing, and consulting ministry of Dr. Frank Thomas and Joyce Thomas. Contact Hope For Life, International, Inc. at www.Hope4Life.net.

Available for purchase:
- The book and workbook for *What's Love Got to Do with It?*: *Love, Power, Sex, & God*
- *They Like To Never Quit Praisin' God: The Role of Celebration in Preaching*
- Sermons by Dr. Thomas
- First-ever preaching class on CD

Also:
- Be part of a book discussion of *What's Love Got To Do with It?*
- View articles and lectures by Dr. Thomas